Black Elk's Story

Black Elk's Story

*Distinguishing
Its Lakota
Purpose*

JULIAN RICE

University of New Mexico Press
Albuquerque

Parts of chapter 7 appeared in "Becoming a Helper: Spirit Guides and Human Growth in Two Lakota Stories," *North Dakota Quarterly* 55.1 (Winter 1987): 137–50.

Parts of chapter 8 appeared in "*Akicita* of the Thunder: Horses in Black Elk's Vision," *MELUS* 12.1 (1985): 5–23.

Materials from The South Dakota Oral History Center at the University of South Dakota in Vermillion were obtained with the assistance of the directors, Herbert Hoover and Leonard Brughier.

Library of Congress Cataloging-in-Publication Data

Rice, Julian, 1940–
    Black Elk's story: distinguishing its Lakota purpose/ Julian Rice.—1st ed.
        p.   cm.
    Includes bibliographical references and index.
    ISBN 0-8263-1262-4
    1. Black Elk, 1863–1950.   2. Oglala Indians—Biography.   3. Oglala Indians—Religion and mythology.   4. Oglala Indians—Philosophy.
    5. Neihardt, John Gneisenau, 1881–1973.   I. Title.
E99.03B5367   1991
978'.004975—dc20   90-27601

To Pete Catches, Sr.
and all Lakota traditionalists
And for my mother, my father,
and Jonathan J. Rice

CONTENTS

INTRODUCTION: Filling in the Blanks   *ix*

CHAPTER ONE: Who was Black Elk?   *1*

CHAPTER TWO: Distancing Black Elk and Neihardt   *15*

CHAPTER THREE: Neihardt's Christian Matrix   *36*

CHAPTER FOUR: Neihardt's Mission and
Black Elk's Center   *48*

CHAPTER FIVE: Shaped by Ritual: The Enactment of
Black Elk's Visions   *65*

CHAPTER SIX: Black Elk and Lakota Healing   *75*

CHAPTER SEVEN: Becoming a Helper   *92*

CHAPTER EIGHT: *Akicita* of the Thunder   *112*

CHAPTER NINE: *Tatanka Iyacin:* To Be like the Buffalo   *125*

CONCLUSION: The Metaphor is the Message   *148*

WORKS CITED   *155*

INDEX   *161*

INTRODUCTION

Filling in the Blanks

Until Raymond J. DeMallie edited the complete transcripts of John G. Neihardt's 1931 and 1944 interviews with Black Elk for the University of Nebraska Press (*The Sixth Grandfather*, 1984), *Black Elk Speaks* was received by most readers as a sacrosanct revelation. DeMallie's presentation and analysis of the manuscripts reveal that Neihardt's poeticizing often involved significant changes of meaning. But even more dramatic changes may have occurred between Black Elk's oral expression in Lakota, its translation into English by his son, Ben, its copying in English by Neihardt's daughter, Hilda, and the interruptions during which translated phrases were queried and revised (DeMallie, intro. to Black Elk, *The Sixth Grandfather* 32). The vocal conventions of oral speech for ceremonial purposes would have supplied nuance, mood, and meaning. The English-only transcripts convey little sense of oral punctuation (e.g., "and then," or "it is said"), or other aesthetic techniques that differentiate literature, poetry, and symbolic narrative from simple reportage in any language. In our attempt to understand Black Elk's words we must admit that the dimension of texture that most makes a text "literature" has been lost. In the absence of a Black Elk videotape, we are as necessarily limited in our grasp of his original intent as we are in the study of the Bible.

The subsuming of their oral tradition in the printed word is not viewed favorably by some Lakota people, but a leading Lakota author, Vine Deloria, Jr., has called for the development of a written theology, derived from Black Elk, that will "someday challenge the Eastern and Western traditions as a way of looking at the world" (intro. to Neihardt, *Black Elk Speaks* xiv). Any such theology will have to be vitalized by disagreement and argument. The views expressed in this book are often directly opposed (and sometimes in agreement with) those of Deloria and other critics. In addition this book does not presume to be an addition to Lakota culture itself but only part of a growing body of written (and forthrightly non-Indian) interpretations of Native American oral expression. Now at least we are past the need to promote tolerance based only on likeness. *Black Elk's Story* intends to present the view that Neihardt and Black Elk are different in ways that comparatively illuminate their separate spiritual traditions. Christian missionaries often emphasize religious differences to show that Lakota people need what only Christianity can offer. The accessibility of *The Sixth Grandfather* makes it possible to appreciate Lakota insights our own culture ignores.

No one has had to sort out religious differences more responsibly than Lakota medicine men of the twentieth century. DeMallie indicates that Black Elk had been a Catholic for nearly thirty years before he spoke to Neihardt in 1931, and yet the transcript presents a Lakota elder still immersed in the traditional religion. To understand his voice as representing a Lakota culture independent of adopted Christianity or imputed archetypes, Black Elk must be cleanly disentangled from Neihardt. Both were religious thinkers, but that does not mean, as several prestigious commentators have assumed, that they were Platonically programmed to be spiritual twins. The thinking of both men is often antithetical, and each in turn regarded the world differently from many modern readers, especially those attuned to the popular ecumenism of a Jung or a Campbell.

Neihardt was a Christian poet in the typological tradition with a strong, consistent view of history as providential progress. His relatively conventional vision foregrounds Platonic dualism and Christian universalism in his epic poetry, and from that standpoint he edited the Black Elk interviews for *Black Elk Speaks*. His literary metaphors and assumptions can be compared to such biblically inspired writers as Milton and Hawthorne, and his commonly noted pathos in depicting the vanishing American is strongly theological. In his view, Native Americans had to be crucified for the sake of their own redemption through God's instrument, the "Aryan" race (on Neihardt's use of "Aryan" for "Indo-European," see Whitney 86).

It is true that in a factual sense Black Elk was also a Christian, but his Christianity appears to have been more social than spiritual. Raised in buffalo hunting days, Black Elk may well have chosen baptism at the age of thirty-seven for a warrior's reasons, to protect the people from persecution, and to help them adjust to reservation life. The biographical record shows him to be an active participant in catechizing other Lakota, in celebrating Christian holidays, and attending Church conferences. In addition, his detailed description of Lakota ceremonies for Joseph Epes Brown in *The Sacred Pipe* (1947) is often overtly Catholic, as if he were trying to make the Lakota religion more acceptable to Christians. In the 1944 Neihardt interviews, on the other hand, Black Elk is rarely Christian and makes many statements diametrically opposed in specific instances to interpretations heavily Christianized only three years later for *The Sacred Pipe*.

The 1931 and 1944 Neihardt interviews present a *wicaśa wakan* (holy man and healer) whose religion is immediately experienced, ritualized, and directed toward physical and spiritual continuance on the earth. Neihardt's religion is other-worldly, celebrating spiritual evolution beyond time, and providence teaching man to anticipate the end of the world as the great day of Creation. In the midst of such contradictions the Black Elk Neihardt missed may be approached in terms of the traditional male obligations he refused to relinquish. Since doctoring in the Indian way was his raison d'être for nearly twenty years, Black Elk will here be given cultural dimension through several accounts of the theory and practice of Lakota medicine. Further perspectives on visionary experience will then be provided. Most of the young men with whom Black Elk grew up sought to establish kinship with supernatural "helpers" in order to become confidence-inspiring defenders and providers. In the stories, "Miwakan Yuhala" 'Sword Owner' and "Hokśila Wan" 'A Boy,' the growth of the "red" power ensuring harmony in the camp circle is traced in the initiatory adventures of two young men who follow the same road that Black Elk traveled for the first half of his life.

But Black Elk was not only a bulwark of social stability, he was an extraordinarily gifted visionary favored with the potentially dangerous power of the Thunder. As a Thunder dreamer, Crazy Horse's power appeared in sudden dramatic bursts that could psychologically immobilize an enemy. While few had this "black" explosiveness, all men like the heroes in the "helper" stories had to be reliably "red," like the buffalo. DeMallie emphasizes that Black Elk was a Thunder dreamer in both of his major visions, but this power is balanced and stabilized by the red buffalo in his Great Vision and in the Buffalo ceremony he helps to enact. Just as it is necessary to look carefully at the meaning of black, especially in relation to the Great Vision, and to understand Black Elk as having a warrior's temperament, so omitting the red side of Black Elk deprives his Thunder vision of its contrasting impact and significance. The meaning of the buffalo for Lakota identity, in the way the people regard themselves and treat each other, will also be examined in several texts to supplement Black Elk's commonplace likening of the Lakota to the buffalo throughout *The Sixth Grandfather.*

While the text of the transcript does not explicitly develop every aspect of Lakota culture, and emphasizes the black power more than the red, the thunder more than the buffalo, Black Elk's account of Lakota culture is still remarkably comprehensive for a single "informant." In regard to his Great Vision in particular, it is natural to doubt that he offers a verbatim report of something experienced at the age of nine. The old Lakota culture was so thoroughly metaphorical that the truth of a vision may be like the truth of literature. The value is not in the metaphor itself, so as to literalize it, but in the process of manifestation to which the truth of any single metaphor is subordinate and relative.

If Black Elk embellished his Vision to make it representative of his mature Lakota memory, his inspiration to do so may itself have been visionary. Black Elk's 1944 story of Sharp Nose the Arapahoe, who worries that he may have "lied" about sacred matters to an enemy in order to restore his people's horses and to make peace, may well be Black Elk's reflection on the literal truth of his narrative. The truth is in the meaning and the effect rather than the time and place of reception or the plane of consciousness—sleeping dream, waking dream, narrative act. Expression is the primary miracle, and its source is supernatural whether it sends a dream, a report of a dream, or a story of a dream.

The present study will introduce several lines of inquiry that the author hopes others will develop further. The social history of *Black Elk Speaks,* no less than its text, necessitates an extensive examination of Neihardt's Christianity, juxtaposing it to analogues from Milton to contemporary Jesuit missionaries on the Lakota reservations; throughout the book significant changes based on Neihardt's religious misunderstandings as he rewrote Black Elk will be noted; Black Elk's own Christianity will be considered both socially and psychologically; Black Elk's traditional male identity as a healer will be placed in the context of Lakota healing practice; his identity as a stable provider and protector will be reflected in several oral narratives of youthful initiation; his particular gift as a Thunder dreamer, especially his sudden inspiration in war and healing, can be understood to define a "black" individuality; while his role as a buffalo man relates him to the "red" order-preserving consistency required of all Lakota men. Finally, symbolic meanings in the Neihardt and Brown interviews are religiously contradictory but spiritually coherent in that Black Elk's metaphors are means of perpetuating, not simply preserving, the Lakota ways.

Black Elk's Story

ONE

Who Was Black Elk?

WIDESPREAD knowledge of Black Elk's life through DeMallie's biography in *The Sixth Grandfather* has made Joseph Epes Brown's question as to who in fact Black Elk really was into more than a search for his "essential qualities" as an abstract holy man (*The Sacred Pipe* xiii). As a representative American Indian adapting to conditions of spiritual occupation, Black Elk struggled to come to terms with the religion that all Indian people were aggressively urged to embrace. During his European tour with Buffalo Bill in 1889 Black Elk wrote two letters to a Presbyterian missionary newsletter for the Sioux, describing his travels and his intent to see the place "where they killed Jesus" (*The Sixth Grandfather* 10). Although he was not then a Christian, he appears to have wished to understand Christianity in the land where it appeared, in the same sense that Lakota sacred places made the occurrence of visions more probable (*The Sixth Grandfather* 10). Perhaps the success of the whites argued for the validity of their religion, or their sustained presence in a place may have brought their spiritual power to that place: "Black Elk told Neihardt that while he was in Europe his own spiritual power disappeared, and perhaps this led him to Christianity. As soon as he returned to Pine Ridge, his power came back to him" (*The Sixth Grandfather* 11).

But Black Elk's power at Pine Ridge was quickly being supplanted by Jesuit missionaries who were changing Lakota land from a visionary matrix to an earthly training ground. During a fourteen year period after his return from Europe, the Jesuits had largely overwhelmed Lakota resistance so that most of the traditional healers like Black Elk had been converted or discredited. In 1904 a Father Lindebner, arriving to administer last rites to a sick boy, discovered Black Elk in the midst of doctoring him. Incensed by this blasphemy, Lindebner threw Black Elk's drum, rattle, and other spiritual objects out of the tent and then seized him by the throat saying predictably, "Satan, get out!" Black Elk submitted abjectly in the report by his daughter, Lucy Looks Twice, herself a staunch Catholic. When the priest emerged, he took Black Elk to Holy Rosary Mission, instructed him for two weeks, and baptized him "Nicholas," in honor of the saint's day, December 6, on which the conversion occurred (*The Sixth Grandfather* 14).

Black Elk's capitulation may appear to have been too immediate to suit those who had admired him in Neihardt's prose. But had Black Elk and others not found channels in Church practice through which to continue Lakota tradition, many Lakota values might not have persisted to fill the traditional forms that once again openly exist (see Amiotte, "Eagles Fly Over" and "Lakota Sun Dance"). Under the circumstances in the early part of the century, Black Elk could not help his people as his upbringing had moved him to do until the age of thirty-seven. As DeMallie points out, almost all reservation people "belonged at least nominally to one or another Christian denomination" (*The Sixth Grandfather* 15). Many aspects of traditional society transformed and persisted. Men's and women's societies, a fundamental source of adult identity became "sodalities," such as St. Mary's or St. Joseph's. For Black Elk and those relatively few others whose lives had been specialized in spiritual matters, the Church offered opportunities for continued ministering to the people within a different set of metaphors, which Black Elk quickly learned and employed. But although he was persuasive enough to have accomplished at least four hundred conversions, according to one estimate (*The Sixth Grandfather* 27) his inner feelings about his work for the Church, as they are expressed in the written record, are anything but consistent.

DeMallie is, therefore, able to imply that Black Elk became a Catholic for reasons of social expediency but remained a traditional Lakota at heart. Although the Jesuits at Holy Rosary Mission were particularly outraged at the epilogue of *Black Elk Speaks,* the prayer to the six grandfathers rather than to God, and "although the old man was embarrassed in front of the priests who had been his confessors and advisors for many years, he never denied the sincerity of his final appeal to the grandfathers" (*The Sixth Grandfather* 58). But more contradictions occur in a retraction, purportedly written and signed by Black Elk after a wagon accident in 1933 serious enough to make him think he was dying: "I called my priest to pray for me and so he gave me Extreme Unction and Holy Eucharist. Therefore I will tell you the truth. Listen, my friends!" (Quoted and retranslated by DeMallie, *The Sixth Grandfather* 59). Black Elk summarizes his conversion, his beliefs, his activity as a catechist, the Christianization of his family and the superiority of the priests to the medicine men: "The Indian medicine men did not stop sin. Now I despise sin. And I want to go straight in the righteous way that the Catholics teach us so my soul will reach heaven" (*The Sixth Grandfather* 60–61).

Nevertheless, Black Elk recovered and spent nearly the next decade teaching non-Indians the value and validity of Lakota culture at an annual pageant in the Black Hills. Inside a canvas tipi with a rainbow painted over the door, Black Elk recreated his healing ceremony including the preparation of his body with paint, the wearing of a buffalo horn headdress and other ornaments, and the singing of his own songs received in visions, accompanied by rattle and drum. DeMallie explains the social context of Black Elk's risking further charges of paganism: "Jesuit missionaries remained firm in their conviction—at least until the 1960s—that Indian religion necessarily represented an earlier, more primitive stage in human history that would have to be completely replaced by Christianity in order for the people to raise themselves to the enlightenment of civilization" (*The Sixth Grandfather* 66). The Lakota were allowed a few cultural teddy bears, such as parade regalia on the fourth of July, to ease their way into the twentieth century and into heaven, but were forbidden to backslide all the way to healing ceremonies or the sun dance, even without piercing as done in the pageant.

In spite of the fact that Black Elk remained a Catholic for the

rest of his life, he spent his last years working actively to preserve the Lakota religion using every available vehicle. It was
during the Duhamel pageant that he taught Reginald and Gladys
Laubin his pipe invocation, which they in turn faithfully repeated in their Indian dance concerts all over the world (*The
Sixth Grandfather* 66); then in 1944 he presented a second, detailed and extensive set of interviews to Neihardt. Finally in
1947 he initiated the preparation of a book on Lakota ceremonies, *The Sacred Pipe,* recorded and edited by Joseph Epes
Brown. Although it has many Christian elements (to be discussed here), *The Sacred Pipe* remains one of the best written descriptions of Lakota ceremonies. In addition to oral and ceremonial traditions, the book has helped to bring about the Lakota
revival now firmly established. Several other biographical reports bolster DeMallie's suggestion that Black Elk never lost his
Lakota consciousness and returned to the Lakota religion near
the end of his life. From 1936 until 1950, the year of his death,
the Laubins never heard Black Elk speak of Catholicism during
their annual visits: "We had the feeling he was interested mainly
in early days" (*The Sixth Grandfather* 71). And in 1948 a young
visitor, Charles Hanson, visiting while Black Elk was confined
to bed, emerged to tell Ben Black Elk that the old man "now
felt he had made a mistake in rejecting [the old religion] for
Christianity" and that it may well have been that the Lakota
religion would have served the people better (*The Sixth Grandfather* 71–72).

While DeMallie selects biographical evidence to suggest that
Black Elk's Christianity had only a temporary phase of deep
sincerity, Michael F. Steltenkamp wrote "No More Screech
Owl" to make known the wishes of Lucy Looks Twice, Black
Elk's last surviving daughter. She told Steltenkamp that Neihardt had refused or neglected to write the last part of Black
Elk's life, although her father had wanted to be remembered "as
a Christian man praying" (Steltenkamp 72). In addition to Lucy's
personal reminiscences of Black Elk riding long distances in the
middle of the night to administer last rites, or his zest in teaching children communion songs in Lakota, other contemporaries
of Black Elk such as John Lone Goose attest to his vigorous

Christianity: "He never talked about the old ways. All he talked about was the Bible and Christ . . . to Indians who didn't know it" (Steltenkamp 107). And far from returning to Lakota religion later in life, Lucy states that Black Elk lived up to his promise "to do away with his early practices" even when other medicine men like Paul Catches (father of contemporary Pine Ridge spiritual leader, Pete Catches) returned to the old ways (Steltenkamp 102).

Steltenkamp quotes Ben Marrowbone to illustrate the thoroughgoing grasp of Christian principles displayed by Black Elk: "The pipe is like the Old Testament: it's a road to take . . . a road of honesty . . . It teaches how to live a good life like the ten commandments" (Steltenkamp 160). But with the arrival of Christ through the missionaries, that prophetic foundation deepens. The Lakota have learned how to elevate heaven and denigrate the earth "This is not our home. Our home is the new world coming" (Steltenkamp 160). The purpose of life is no longer to protect one's own on earth but to "save ourselves and to see our [dead] relatives again" (Steltenkamp 160). The resemblance between Black Elk as a Lakota Christian and as a Ghost dancer is unmistakable. On his Christian road, Black Elk looks for happy endings beyond the present world, a consummation devoutly to be wished by the Jesuits and by Steltenkamp, who interprets as well as reports on Black Elk's life. In one of his more vivid analogues Steltenkamp views Black Elk's conversion experience as providentially rough:

> Judaism's Saul was enroute to Damascus so as to persecute Christians when, all of a sudden, he was knocked off his horse and blinded (through Divine intervention—eventually changing his name (to Paul) and religious practice (to Christianity) . . . Knowing this Bible story, Lucy agreed that her father's experience was like Paul's, i.e., being thrown out of the tent was his equivalent to falling off a horse. (Steltenkamp 96)

While DeMallie implies a conversion of expedience and Steltenkamp offers a fortunate fall, Clyde Holler does not believe that a conversion in any meaningful sense ever occurred.

Instead of making Black Elk a traditionalist at heart or a consistently progressive Catholic, Holler sees Black Elk as equally Christian and Lakota: "Black Elk's commitment to Christianity does not necessarily imply any lessening of his commitment to traditional Lakota religion" (39). When Black Elk compares the pipe with Christ in *The Sacred Pipe,* Holler points out, "Christ does not replace the pipe; both have co-equal validity" (42). The subsequent account of the seven rites makes many Christian analogies in order to assert the "equality of traditional religion with Christianity" and to bring those rites back again in a more acceptable (Christianized) form but still basically as themselves. Black Elk changes the sun dance, Holler writes, away from a traditional prayer for individual recovery or success into a Lakota version of spiritual sacrifice and world renewal. Thus he has not Christianized so much as modernized the ceremony, making it acceptable to partially assimilated Lakota and feasible in the white man's world. All this is a conscious strategy on Black Elk's part, consistent with protecting the people's spiritual life and self-respect in changing conditions. For Holler, Black Elk became a Catholic to find metaphors that would infuse the Lakota religion with life and assure its continuance. In the process he developed sincere respect for Christianity but never to the point that he believed Christianity to be deeper than a Lakota "foundation."

Holler's case for a bicultural Black Elk rings truest in relation to the text of *The Sacred Pipe.* While the Lakota ceremonies are described in authentic detail corresponding to other accounts recorded around the turn of the century (Densmore, Dorsey, Fletcher, and Walker), they are balanced by an often excessive Christian commentary. Black Elk consciously tries to make Lakota religion expressive of the same truths as Christianity, while Brown in his footnotes shows Lakota symbolism to be as profound as that of the "great world religions." In the book's foreward, Black Elk implies that he exemplifies the missionary belief that the righteous heathens would be converted before the Last Judgment and that the end of the world is near, a belief foreign to Lakota culture prior to the Ghost Dance, itself a Christiantized religion.

The fear of damnation for the individual as well as the whole earth formulates Black Elk's interpretations of the red and black roads, to be discussed later in this book. In *The Sacred Pipe* Black Elk turns the red road of peace into the straight and narrow path to heaven and the black road of difficulty into the path of error and destruction (7n). The last is the road to nowhere in the Platonic sense imposed by Neihardt on the Black Elk of *Black Elk Speaks*. The Christian Black Elk, or Brown's Black Elk, similarly identifies the Ghost Keeping ceremony as a purgatorial warning to all who behold it: "He who is well prepared is he who knows that he is nothing compared with *Wakan-Tanka,* who is everything; then he knows that world which is real" (8).

Consistent with the unreality-of-the-earth concept, Brown helpfully quotes a Blackfoot Sioux declaring his understanding of what must have been for him the essence of Christianity: "We raise our hands (when we pray) because we are wholly dependent on the Great Spirit; it is His liberal hand that supplies all our wants. We strike the ground afterward, because we are miserable beings, worms crawling before His face" (In Chittenden and Richardson, *De Smet* 253, qtd. in Brown 14). Whereas the earth is the abode of worms, darkness (a profound source of revelation in the *inipi* [sweat lodge] and other ceremonies) takes on the Christian meanings of sin and ignorance throughout *The Sacred Pipe:* "It is your will that the peoples of the world do not live in the darkness of ignorance" (65). In another emphatically Christian image, perhaps the major metaphor of Neihardt's epic poetry, God is "eternal light," and the sun dance honors "the grace of *Wakan-Tanka*" by which all creatures are enlightened (71).

Christian imagery is especially abundant in the sun dance section because of the obvious opportunity to draw parallels between the piercing and the crucifixion. In the sun dance the "flesh represents ignorance," so that the people can be "freed from the bonds of the flesh." Nothing in traditional Lakota religion would define the physical body as evil, and in *The Sacred Pipe* even the buffalo, the spirit of protectiveness and generosity, becomes "the earth" in a purely physical sense, and therefore something to be transcended after passing acknowledgement (91).

Christian rhetoric also overtakes the black face paint worn by the dancers. Black is the color of inevitable difficulty, as well as the courage inseparable from it, in many Lakota expressions. In the 1931 Neihardt transcript, just before his concluding prayer from Harney Peak, Black Elk defines the purpose of a *wicaśa wakan* (sacred man) as bringing the people "out of the black road into the red road" (*The Sixth Grandfather* 293), out of their poverty and despair and back to Lakota consciousness. In *The Sacred Pipe* black incongruously becomes "the color of ignorance" while the black facial stripes are specifically "the bonds which tie us to the earth . . . when we tear ourselves away from the thongs, it is as if the spirit were liberated from our dark bodies" (92). The corresponding footnote quotes Black Elk, adding: "By going on the warpath, we know that we have done something bad, and we wish to hide our faces from *Wakan-Tanka*" (92). Only three years earlier, Black Elk had told Neihardt that the warriors painted their faces black to celebrate a successful raid or horse taking. Their relatives would also "paint their faces black and then dance. When we whip Germany, we will all black our faces" (*The Sixth Grandfather* 317).

Thus far we can see three Black Elks from the biographical record and from the text edited by Brown: 1) a Black Elk who was a sincere Catholic but who returned to Lakota religion after the Neihardt interviews; 2) a consistently active and committed Catholic who never turned back; and 3) an ingenious, syncretic Lakota-Christian. It may be that all three images are equally true. Writers go through many phases of thought and easily differentiated periods of expression. Of Black Elk's major works, *The Sacred Pipe* is the most consistently Christian. *Black Elk Speaks* has several implicitly Christian additions and changes made by the psychologically Christian Neihardt. The most purely Lakota and non-Christian Black Elk texts comprise the body of material collected in *The Sixth Grandfather,* including the 1930–31 interviews which became *Black Elk Speaks* and the 1944 interviews, some of which became Neihardt's later novel *When the Tree Flowered.* In a passage from 1931, watered down

8

later by Neihardt, Black Elk is sharply critical of missionary influence and clearly angry about their wrongfully imposed suppression: "today I feel very sorry—I could just cry—to see my people in a muddy water, dirty with the bad acts of the white people . . . All of our religion of the old times that the early Indians had was left behind them as they fled and the water covered the region" (*The Sixth Grandfather* 289).

He answers the oft-repeated Jesuit dictum that traditional religion was devil worship with unintimidated directness: "The whites think we have the power from the devil, but I'll say that they probably have that themselves" (*The Sixth Grandfather* 289). And he goes on to say that Christians had no message of love for Indians that Indians did not already practice. In fact the Lakota were overcome because they actually practiced their religion and honored their treaties, while the whites used both to implement betrayal. Black Elk pointedly invokes the golden rule, the distinctive "contribution" of the religion preached by hypocrites:

> The first thing an Indian learns is to love each other and that they should be relative-like to the four-leggeds. The next thing is telling the truth. Whatever they say, they stand by it. Here's where the Indians made their mistake. We should treat our fellowmen all alike—the Great Spirit made men all alike. Therefore, we made a mistake when we tried to get along with the whites. We tried to love them as we did ourselves. On account of this we are now in misery. They were men like us . . . Because we Indians were relatives to the four-leggeds, we wanted to get along with them. But now we see that the white race has done great wrong to the Indians. (*The Sixth Grandfather* 289–90)

Within this "wrong," Black Elk himself was most directly affected by aggressive missionaries. In describing his first successful cure, Black Elk adds that long before Father Lindebner, another Roman Catholic priest disrupted one of his healing ceremonies and confiscated the ritual objects: "Not long after this, the Black Robe fell off his horse and died. The patient of this ceremony was cured anyway" (*The Sixth Grandfather* 239).

Apart from the literal truth of retribution, perhaps this was Black Elk's answer to the Christian conviction that Lakota religion was nearly extinct. In this instance, Black Elk apparently felt that missionaries who interfere will only harm themselves, while the Lakota ways remain alive and well.

Although his opinions of whites and their religion changed dramatically at times, the purpose of his speech, as defender and spokesman for the people, never changed. Black Elk's identity had been formed within the hoop. He was not only a nineteenth century Lakota warrior until he was almost thirty, he was a practicing *wicaśa wakan* until the age of thirty-seven. Though he spent many years after 1904 as a Catholic missionary, Steltenkamp's idea that he made a complete transition to twentieth century Catholic consciousness is improbable. Habitual ways of thought would have had to be erased, not simply dismissed as a wrongful creed. Black Elk may not have wished to adopt any aspect of the white man's culture. As late as 1944 he told Neihardt that Crazy Horse was greater than Red Cloud or Spotted Tail because he never "left for the white man . . . Crazy Horse is the last big chief, and then it's all over" (*The Sixth Grandfather* 322). But while he inwardly refused to surrender, as implied by his admiration for Crazy Horse, he lived more in the manner of Spotted Tail, who was not the cowardly compromiser portrayed by Neihardt. His report of Black Elk's youthful response to the Brulé leader is not in the transcript:

> I saw him and I did not like him. He was fat with Waśichu food and we were lean with famine. My father told me that he came to make his nephew [Crazy Horse] surrender to the soldiers, because our own people had turned against us . . . How could men get fat by being bad and starve by being good? (*Black Elk Speaks* 138)

Actually Black Elk followed Spotted Tail's lead in helping his people to live. Both had travelled widely in the white man's world and knew the folly of active resistance against irrational aggression. Under the gun for several decades during the early reservation period, Spotted Tail kept liquor away from his camp, maintained an annual sun dance and buffalo hunt as long as possible, and crushed troublemakers who would have given the army an excuse to slaughter his people (Poole 80, 89–93, 188; Hyde 308–10). Like Sitting Bull he never became a Christian and he steadfastly resisted federal pressure to accept agriculture as a more advanced way to live (Hyde 255, 299–300; Poole 116–17, 181–87; Vestal, *Sitting Bull* 272).

Making only such compromises as were absolutely necessary, Spotted Tail understood the value of presenting the whites with an image of intelligence and charm, much as Black Elk did in the books he actively sought to write. Both Black Elk and Spotted Tail used language persuasively to achieve long-term benefits for their people. In his 1944 story of Sharp Nose, the Arapahoe (*The Sixth Grandfather* 371–76), the hero restores his tribe's horses because he presents a fiction to the Crow thieves. They are so moved by the "sacred bundle" Sharp Nose has resourcefully invented that the two tribes forge a permanent alliance. Regardless of what Sharp Nose actually believed about the bundle, he was seeking to ensure his own tribe's future, the truth of the "sacred" demonstrated by its healing effect rather than its intrinsic meaning.

Even Crazy Horse adjusted as much he could before he died. He agreed to help the army fight the Nez Percé and was seeking to allay his reputation as a troublemaker and simply survive, just before he was killed (Ambrose 467–69). Wishing to protect those he cared for from injury or death, Black Elk presented overt compromise while retaining the ideal of not "going over." An older contemporary, Joseph White Bull, underwent the same tensions even more severely than Black Elk. A strong resister of land sales on the Standing Rock reservation, the reknowned warrior spent three months in solitary confinement at the age of fifty-two because he would not agree to a low price for grazing rights on his land (Vestal, *Warpath* 241). Although he was a member of the Congregational Church, he had a dream after his conversion that suggests a return to his pre-Christian beliefs. In the dream of April 1907, a buffalo skeleton emerges from the ground and gradually becomes covered with flesh. It then directs White Bull to some healing roots, a promise, perhaps, of restoration for Lakota culture, following its debilitating suppression by the government and the Church (Vestal, *Warpath* 249–50).

White Bull was one of the great warriors of his generation, and on a changed field of battle he held firm. Black Elk was a warrior as well, his role as a healer and director of ceremonies being inseparable in the old Lakota culture from his role as a warrior. As in warfare, he could be deceptive when he had to be, but the determination of when he is sincere and when not cannot be absolutely known. Rather than attempt to determine what Black Elk meant, it may be more instructive to attempt to interpret what he said, even if his words in different contexts are not consistent with our sense of great religious leaders unfolding a sequential teaching.

While Neihardt reduced the warrior references in Black Elk's story, DeMallie has shown that the Great Vision came from the Thunder beings, making Black Elk preeminently effective at renewing life in situations of conflict or illness. But if this was Black Elk's individualized power, as other men had power from the bear, the wolf, and many other *wamakaśkan* (animal spirits), every Lakota male was continually reminded to be a *tatanka* (buffalo bull). In the Custer fight, the skirmishes after Wounded Knee, and the missionary assault on the dignity and worth of Lakota culture, Black Elk stood up for the people as a bull defends the herd. Even when that effort was ideologically inconsistent, its purpose and energy remained the same. Through *The Sacred Pipe* he attempted to make survival conditions for Lakota consciousness and self esteem favorable in an overwhelmingly Christian world.

When he was not confronting that world to make an alliance favorable to the Lakota in the manner of Spotted Tail, he turned inward to joke with his family, celebrate Christian holidays (Lakota rites were forbidden), and tell children bible stories (they could be whipped in school for even speaking of their traditions) (Steltenkamp 107–8). Though the life Steltenkamp describes was externally Christian, Black Elk upheld relationships that were definitely Lakota even if the mythology and the symbolism, for the sake of the children under conditions of occupation, were necessarily Christian. The extensive efforts to convey

Lakota culture to the future manifest the endurance highly prized in a warrior (Hassrick 34). Black Elk may have looked ineffectual at times, but in terms of the values learned in the hoop he lived as a man should, creating joy among his relatives, including his daughter, Lucy, who wished to preserve the Catholic father and the home he made for her in the twentieth century. On the other hand, the written record reveals a many-faceted thinker, assuming a range of powers from those of the lightning to those of the elk, and yet through each change remaining a *tatanka,* defender and generator of the nation's life.

And while one can follow this steady persistence through Black Elk's thought and action, the original transcripts of *The Sixth Grandfather* give a fundamentally more vigorous and fully human Black Elk than the polished texts. When Black Elk says the black horse of his vision neighed so loud it could be heard "all over the universe like a radio" (*The Sixth Grandfather* 133), we get a sense of his adaptability, his refusal to vanish. Perhaps Neihardt removed this to preserve his portrait of the "old prophet" (introduction to the 1972 Pocket Books edition xiii), who could be bitter but only with heaviness, never with the teasing tone present even in his vision-talk:

> Again I looked toward the people and took good notice this time. I saw there were some animals [people?] in there of different tribes that I was to get along with on earth. I wasn't quite sure yet whether I saw a white man or not. (What I saw there actually happened, for now I have friends of all the different tribes, even of the whites . . .). (*The Sixth Grandfather* 138–39)

The text of *The Sixth Grandfather* is a better text than *Black Elk Speaks* because it has not been oversimplified. It retains a greater range of mood and experience spoken by a more authentic voice. Of course Black Elk speaks to Neihardt in Lakota, and *The Sixth Grandfather* is largely the translation of his son, Ben Black Elk, except where Neihardt halted the process to elaborate and rephrase (*The Sixth Grandfather* 32). If *Black Elk Speaks* in English is "told through John G. Neihardt," perhaps *The Sixth Grandfather* should properly be "told through Ben

Black Elk." Future students of the Black Elk material will find the latter text to have the ironies, reversals, and shifts of voice found in most of the Western literature now considered worthy of extended thought and comment. *Black Elk Speaks,* on the other hand, may perhaps be relegated to the ranks of nineteenth century curios, reflecting white misconceptions of Indians. Additional reasons for preferring *The Sixth Grandfather* will be examined, as Neihardt's Christian assumptions and Black Elk's Lakota context are brought forward in subsequent chapters.

TWO

Distancing Black Elk
and Neihardt

Even before DeMallie's publication of *The Sixth Grand-father*, the transcripts of the interviews with Black Elk, from which John Neihardt fashioned *Black Elk Speaks* and *When the Tree Flowered*, discrepancies between the manuscript copies (Neihardt Collection, University of Missouri) and the book caused admirers of Neihardt to assume a defensive stance. In the preface to the only edition currently in print, Vine Deloria, Jr. is more emphatic in his praise than is usually felt to be necessary when he describes "the only religious classic of this century," and its "eloquent message." Though he does not name them, Deloria refutes scholars who "have said that the book reflects more of Neihardt than it does of Black Elk" (*Black Elk Speaks* xiv). The existence of such skepticism may have prompted Deloria to overcompensate in his use of uncritical adjectives, for his answer to the skeptics is as uncharacteristic of Deloria in his other writings as parts of *Black Elk Speaks* are uncharacteristic of Neihardt in the body of his poetry. Deloria simply asserts that Neihardt's relationship to Black Elk need not be questioned because both men are attuned to a transcendent wisdom that causes their personalities to become "indistinguishable" (xiv). Seeking to bury the distinction between Black Elk's Lakota understanding and Neihardt's Christian metaphors, Deloria evokes Mark Antony's attempt to restore Caesar to a pedestal from which Shakespeare had unsentimentally removed him: "great religious teachings . . . encompass everyone who understands them and personalities become indistinguishable from the transcendent truth that is expressed. So let it be with *Black Elk Speaks*" (xiv). In defining a "classic," Deloria is notably Western in his paraphrase and comparison. Like Shakespeare, the ultimate paragon, Neihardt has achieved universality, the be-all and end-all of literary effort: "It encourages us to emphasize the best that dwells within us . . . It is good. It is enough" (xiv).

If, on the other hand, Black Elk and Neihardt are not thought to be emissaries from the same celestial home but human beings shaped by two vastly different cultures, their unexamined equation is neither good nor enough. Later in this study Neihardt's epic poetry will be shown to be not only Western but self-consciously Christian in conception and expression. In the context of Neihardt's other work, the changes that he made in adapting the interviews to the book can be understood as ideological and sectarian rather than simply ecumenical. Disentangling Neihardt from Black Elk can also clarify more of the latter's Lakota message and purpose.

Some of the strongest support for separating Neihardt and Black Elk may be derived from the proponent of their fusion just quoted. In his 1979 book *The Metaphysics of Modern Existence,* published in the same year as his Preface to *Black Elk Speaks,* Deloria refers repeatedly to the Platonic dualism of Western peoples, "the belief that ultimate reality exists over and above the transitory experiences of daily life" (19). The Greek aversion to the natural world became a formative determinant of Christianity: "God existed in the Heavenly City where the faithful would be rewarded by eternal life, and all values of importance became those of the other world" (20). Deloria then quotes Gregory Bateson as to the consequences of human self-disparagement:

> If you put God outside and set him vis-à-vis his creation and if you have the idea that you are created in his image, you will logically and naturally see yourself as outside and against the things around you . . . The environment will seem to be yours to exploit. Your survival unit will be you

and your folks or conspecifics against the environment of other social units, other races and the brutes and vegetables. (Bateson 462, qtd. in *Metaphysics* 20).

Deloria goes on to explain how such a *contemptus mundi* attitude had to be replaced or life would have no value. The replacements, nationalism and historical progress, focus the conscious mind on the task of justifying the present within a program of social revolution or, as with Neihardt, within "a divine plan . . . coordinating each and every event preparatory to a grand climactic judgment" (20).

The compelled, fearful intellection Deloria summarizes energized the subjugation of non-Europeans all over the world. Far from perceiving this phenomenon with the distance brought by Bateson or Deloria, Neihardt was an enthusiastic singer of this "historical" process, and his philosophy was part of that Euro-American arrogance that has infected even literary "giants" from Mark Twain (Nigger Jim, Injun Joe) to T. S. Eliot ("Sweeney Among the Nightingales"). His racial theory was typically romantic but unabashedly self-serving:

We might liken the ancient Aryan spirit to a prairie fire driven by an east wind out of Mesopotamia and destined to burn across the world. Now it flared into Persia, and the gloom of the past is still painted with that flare. Now it was a white radiance in Greece, the clear illumination of which still guides the feet of men. Now it burned ruddily in Rome, spread around the Mediterranean, and became as a golden noonday to all the known world. Then it drove northward and lit Europe with a succession of illuminations. (Preface to *The Splendid Wayfaring* [1920] qtd. in Whitney 86)

Neihardt's racism is fortified not by Darwin but by deific plan, and he celebrates "the poetic, imaginative, and forceful spirit that he sees as the creative source behind the works of Western civilization from the *Iliad* to the Conestoga wagon" (Whitney 86).

It is unlikely that Deloria would agree to fuse himself with Neihardt in this matter, nor could he wish a similar fate for

Black Elk. Opposed to Neihardt's theory of a master race, more inventive, alert, and energetic, is Deloria's conception of all species having

> equal status before the presence of the universal power to which all are subject. The religious requirement for all life-forms is thus harmony, and this requirement holds for every species, ours included . . . If ever there were a truly evolutionary theological position, primitive peoples would represent it. (Deloria, *Metaphysics* 153–54)

But in spite of philosophical and spiritual differences that upon examination appear to be profound, Deloria, like most of the other essayists in *A Sender of Words: Essays in Memory of John G. Neihardt,* lauds Neihardt as an oracle speaking from "a reservoir hidden deep within ourselves" and as "an intellectual mountain man, searching through unknown and uncharted landscapes to see what hidden wonders lay before the human mind" (4).

That a man of Deloria's analytical acumen should use this kind of language at all attests to the fondness in which *Black Elk Speaks* has been held for the last twenty-five years. Even Raymond DeMallie, the most thoroughly informed expositor of the differences between Black Elk and Neihardt, joins the chorus of unmitigated praise for Neihardt's spiritual and aesthetic gifts. Like Deloria, DeMallie praises Neihardt for giving the Lakota a universal human identity so that "they seem like real people to readers of all races" ("Lakota Legacy" 110). The criterion for literary excellence as universality is appropriate to the universalism of Neihardt's Christian message. But that message is not ecumenical in the ways that Deloria and DeMallie perceive it.

For Neihardt, different races were not innately equal in their humanity but potentially gathered in by their acceptance of Christ. Neihardt's initial purpose in visiting Black Elk was to gather information on the Ghost Dance, which he eventually portrayed at length in *The Song of the Messiah*. Later in this book, the poem will be analyzed in detail to show that Neihardt considered the Messiah movement to be a benevolent transition to Christian enlightenment. The progression through defeat, and the loss of the Lakota traditional culture, are tragic only in the sense that the crucifixion is tragic. Pain and suffering are suffused by the heavenly light of universal love. DeMallie interprets the Wounded Knee ending, in which Big Foot cries out "my brother" to the soldier who is about to kill him, as the overcoming of "petty differences that separate Indians from whites" ("Lakota Legacy" 126). Because he does not attend to its heavy typological imagery, DeMallie thinks the poem celebrates "the power of the common human spirit" rather than the power of providence. After a similar passing over of Neihardt's biblical and Platonic additions to *Black Elk Speaks,* DeMallie can conclude: "the book never steps outside of Lakota culture" ("Lakota Legacy" 124).

Further analysis of Neihardt's work in this study will show how remarkable it was for a man of Neihardt's literary thinking to understand Black Elk as well as he did. Even more remarkable is how much of the original Black Elk he preserved. With the publication of *The Sixth Grandfather,* the stenographic record of the interviews provides not only a closer approximation to what Black Elk actually says but a better literary text, if Victorian critical standards are not applied. Black Elk's voice in the transcript shows a greater range of emotion and expression. Neihardt's voice in the visionary sections sound like an Old Testament prophet speaking King James English. Elsewhere, virtually all traces of the irony and banter characteristic of male Lakota humor have been dropped. In the biographical sections Neihardt often sounds like Huckleberry Finn, especially when he has Black Elk complain of white betrayal. These changes of tone and meaning are significant but less misleading than the completely invented words which Neihardt puts in Black Elk's mouth. Most of the idealized story of Crazy Horse was derived by Neihardt from written sources so that the Oglala leader is presented as a Platonic philosopher king, who steps far "outside Lakota culture."

Neihardt's social attitudes are conventionally assimilationist. Lakota culture is praised sincerely for what it never was in order to prove that the Indians were fully human and worthy of becoming Americans. Neihardt does not celebrate Lakota culture

19

so much as he praises its passing, as a lesson in the theatre of God's Judgments. Now that the "dark" superstitions of Crazy Horse and Sitting Bull have receded (see subsequent discussion of *The Song of the Indian Wars,* chapter 4), it is time for contemporary Lakota to come to the light. He therefore called for the termination of the reservation system, apparently feeling that Lakota culture and Lakota people had had their day: "They are mostly just poor people living together in a land that cannot support them all, and laboring under psychological, social, and economic handicaps. It is not their 'Indianhood,' as we used to say, but their humanhood that matters" (qtd. in DeMallie, "Lakota Legacy" 130–31).

This concept of benevolence is one of two priorities that most distinguish Neihardt from Black Elk and Christianity from Lakota culture. Christianity has traditionally had a mission to bring one religion to the whole world. This need for psychological validity, confirmed by causing other people to surrender theirs, has softened into modern ecumenism. Human beings evolved by emphasizing their likenesses and minimizing their differences. A tribal religion, on the other hand, is concentrated upon the physical and cultural survival of one people. The other major difference between Neihardt and Black Elk is the dualism defined here by Deloria. The universalist unifies in order to transcend physical mortality. The tribal religions seek continuity in succeeding generations on the earth.

In his introduction to *The Sixth Grandfather* DeMallie writes exclusively as an anthropologist of the Lakota, showing how Neihardt adapted or inadvertently distorted Lakota culture through both design and ignorance. Most notably, DeMallie describes the extent to which Black Elk's Great Vision was specifically a Thunder vision, what this meant, and what was lost through Neihardt's changes. Apparently believing that Black Elk would be less sympathetic for having a large proportion of warrior powers, Neihardt made the Great Vision one of Aristotelian balance. The metaphorical meaning of purification, of thunder as both destroyer and bringer of life, was not recognized by Neihardt as the most distinguished warrior virtue in Lakota culture. But in spite of this oversight, ignorance, or "editing," consciously or unconsciously based on cultural differences, DeMallie offers the obligatory testimonial: "Neihardt was an extraordinarily faithful spokesman for Black Elk; what he wrote was an interpretation of Black Elk's life, but not one that was embellished in any way. Instead, he tried to write what he thought the old man himself would have expressed" (*The Sixth Grandfather* 51).

This "quality" is not simply that of a spiritually sensitive artist but that of a man of the "West," who accepted the doctrine of Manifest Destiny as it grew out of the Christian tradition of physical expansion in the name of God. Neihardt is speaking of more than linguistic translation when he says "the translation— or rather the *transformation*—of what was given me was expressed so that it could be understood by the white world" (*The Sixth Grandfather* 52). "Transformation" in the religious vocabulary Neihardt knew usually meant change to something better, i.e., Black Elk's speech in Lakota foreshadowed its incarnation in Neihardt's scriptured prose. In his 1971 Preface to the Pocket Books edition Neihardt's language still expresses this conception of Black Elk as prefiguring a providential dispensation of light completed only through the translation of his vision into eight languages: "The old prophet's wish is actually being fulfilled" (xiii). Although Black Elk himself (again in Neihardt's religious English) felt he had "fallen away" and had "done nothing," Neihardt is assured that providence will spread the light until the noonday of the final Judgment. Black Elk has a promise to proclaim: "Perhaps with his message spreading across the world he has not failed" (1972 Preface xiii).

Neihardt's intent to bring the good news of the great day is apparent in all his published works. His first epic poem, *The Divine Enchantment,* was inspired by a Jesuit missionary, Louis Jacolliot, who embellished his persuasive rhetoric by finding Christian analogues to the Hindu religion, so as to achieve a smooth transition in the conversion process. *The Bible in India* "suggested to Neihardt [a] use of this tale comparable to that of the Immaculate Conception" (Black 206). In Neihardt's poem, the Hindu and Christian cultures are analagous, but the Christian assumption has always been that God intends such parallels to establish the greater maturity of Christianity. Neihardt's Krishna is Hindu only in the sense that the poet implies a mystical synchronicity of the sounds, "Krishna" and "Christ." "Christna the Messiah" is born of a virgin to spread the "lotus-dream" among mankind. Neihardt described his last work, *The Song of the Messiah,* in such a way as to underscore a thirty-five-year span of Christian emphasis in his epic poetry, and although the meaning of "Indian" changes from the *Enchantment* to the *Song,* both are "retellings of the universal Christ story in an unfamiliar medium" (Neihardt letter, qtd. in Black 210).

In *Black Elk Speaks* and *The Song of the Messiah* the Lakota people are providentially crucified to bring greater love and wisdom to elect witnesses all over the world. As the Christ-like Bigfoot says while he approaches death at Wounded Knee, "'Great Spirit, give us eyes,'/ He prayed, 'to see how sorrow can be wise,/ And pain a sacred teaching that is kind,/ Until the blind shall look upon the blind/ And see one face; until their wounds shall ache/ One holy wound, and all the many wake/ One Being, older than all pain and prayer'" (*Messiah* 95). But universalizing with Christian intent is not more prevalent in Neihardt's work than the dualizing that helps man to see beyond the physical world. Whitney writes of Neihardt's transcendentalism, following Emerson's belief that nature is a symbol of spirit, and the physical is a mere doorway to the essential (*Neihardt* 27–30). In Transcendentalism, as well as in Platonism and Christianity, symbols exist to link the real world with the ideal. According to Neihardt, the highest human utterance makes people aware that the physical body "is a mere skeleton . . . and that some spirit lives among those dry bones" (Neihardt, 1921 speech, qtd. in Whitney 30).

In early stories Neihardt's dualism romanticizes the alienation of the "higher" poetic soul from the grossly material human majority. The absurdly sensitive Omaha Indian protagonist of "The Singer of the Ache" is cast out from his tribe because he refuses to divert energy from the pursuit of his art into mundane activities such as hunting and governing. He is posthumously vindicated, however, when his songs live on to provide comfort during a famine (Aly, "Trappers and Indians" 76).

Lakota and Omaha societies valued songs without being driven to need consolation, but Neihardt's story serves to foreshadow the implication that Black Elk is touched by God and far superior to most of his people. A man with spiritual power, especially the gift of songs, could never have been scorned for ignoring his "civic" duties. Songs were not invented by the gifted poet but received exactly as sent by spirits (Densmore 59). A man who "sang" repeated what he had been given, and the whole tribe valued nothing more than these gifts.

In another story, "The White Wakunda," a spiritually superior Omaha leaves his tribe and learns the gospel, which he attempts to preach upon his return. But when he cannot heal a smallpox epidemic, his benightedly material tribesmen bind him to a post where he is whipped to death, being thereafter mourned by a woman he has named "Mary" (Aly 82). The story fosters the frontier captivity myth in which white Christians were martyred by superstitious savages connecting their foreign presence to sickness or hunger. Neihardt habitually separates a compassionate universal faith from a vengeful tribalism. His cumulative purpose is to bring the world to an essentially Christian vision of unity.

DeMallie sees Black Elk's purpose as fundamentally identical to Neihardt's: "each in his own way strove for the higher understanding that promises to unite mankind in common endeavor" (*The Sixth Grandfather* 67). Clyde Holler has been more forthright than DeMallie in setting down fundamental differences between Neihardt and Black Elk. In his probable mind-set as healer and warrior, considering himself Lakota first and self-consciously "human" not at all, Black Elk, according to Holler hoped that his own people "as a whole" would benefit if readers of *Black Elk Speaks* came to treat them with respect ("Lakota Religion" 26). Holler concentrates on the ritual context of the interviews to support the idea that the narrative was spoken as a healing ritual, to revive the Lakota consciousness, while Neihardt independently concentrated on "transcendental truth," as he did in his prior and subsequent work.

While Holler develops his conception of Black Elk's purpose in terms of the anthropological record, comparing his metaphors to other Lakota sacred men (Fools Crow, Plenty Wolf, and Lame Deer), Arnold Krupat is one of the few to comment on Neihardt as a Victorian poet of the Tennysonian type. Krupat points to Neihardt's overemphasis on Black Elk's supernormal powers, particularly his bringing of rain in the epilogue to conclude that the poet celebrates "the triumphant idealism of romance," miracles for their own sake rather than the amelioration of tribal suffering (132). Krupat then convincingly places Neihardt's Black Elk within Northrop Frye's definition of the romance hero: "superior in degree to other men" and, most particularly, "to his environment" (134). This is exactly the portrait of the spiritually gifted heroes of Neihardt's early stories, "The White Wakunda" and "The Singer of the Ache."

As for their mystical compatibility, both Neihardt and Black Elk believed in a spirit world based on immediate experience rather than wishful belief. But while the Christian mystic receives a vision to bring his flock closer to God, a Lakota vision feeds a community enduring on the earth. Redemption is a European concept still vivid in those who now say that material equality is the heaven to be sought, while the spiritual world is an illusion with no future. Black Elk believed in a spirit world parallel to rather than above this world. Lakota culture did not meditate upon heaven as a sinless, perfect place but sharpened its perceptions so as not to miss the presence on earth of giving spirits manifested continually in each generation. Lakota spiritual belief is as different from Western materialism as it is from Western idealism. Arising in a vastly different social context, Marxism attempted to replace religion within the thought patterns of that same religion.

In Christianity the world is given to the devil, but the New Jerusalem awaits the saved after death. In Marxism the world is given to aristocrats and corporate brutes, but the people will eventually reclaim a classless earth. In the more democratic tradition of Lakota society, visionary power was not used to consolidate monarchy but to sustain the whole people, much as a hunter shared his kill with anyone in need. Marxism replaces the dualism of Christian society with its own dualism of matter and spirit, by valorizing matter. In European culture the deity is conceived of as a royal presence who must be flattered and appeased in prayer, a proper subject to overthrow and replace. In Lakota culture the spirits who provide metaphorical and material food for the people are reciprocally fed in various ceremonies (see Densmore 82, 84 and *The Sacred Pipe* 27). The Lakota asks for "pity" from the spirits, not to demean himself but to recall the kinship tie by which he himself would help a relative in need. Lakota religion requires neither transcendence nor replacement because the spirits are relatives rather than despots.

While Neihardt wished Black Elk to teach him of the other world, Black Elk's narrative speaks of both worlds, though De-Mallie mistakenly thinks that the real world is expressed as a steadily downward spiral after the Great Vision (*The Sixth Grandfather* 55). The Great Vision is always present throughout the historical unfolding, ready at any moment to be remembered, reenacted, read, and told. It represents human wisdom, while Black Elk's life tells of the inevitable suffering that all people undergo. It is the way things are, neither a decline nor an ascent but wisdom both enduring and unfolding in time. Such wholeness has always been best expressed in the intricate subtlety and detail of a concentrated tradition. One is more likely to be deepened by Melville or Faulkner than by Joseph Campbell. The metaphorical detail and abundance of varied expressions contradict the missionaries' assumption that the Lakota are simplistically physical in their ritual practice. Also contradicted is the Marxist zeal to save traditional societies from an "imprisoning . . . resignation" to bring them the gospel of "development, modernization, social justice, and self-reliance" (Novak 130, 137-38, qtd. in Barsh 202).

Traditional Lakota people pray because they are *not* resigned. Prayer is an active seeking of what the west calls "inspiration." The artist prays ritually by acquiring and practicing his technique. Although each act of practice does not result in an inspired work, the artist is not practicing because he is resigned to rational failure but because his rational practice will eventually bring unpredictable results, beyond specific cause and effect paradigms. Writing may result in poetry. Praying may result in a vision. Neither effort is passive, and for the Lakota in particular all such symbolic acts are undertaken tentatively. On the other hand, "capitalists and Marxists believe that Man can recreate himself and become God by subjugating nature, and like Christians they are 'aggressively missionary-minded'" (Barsh 206).

The hatred of the physical world finding expression in the most seminal western thinkers from Plato through Paul to Augustine to Calvin reaches into the philosophies of Freud and Marx. Freud thought of nature as a tooth and claw battle of beasts, and of human nature in a state of continual war with an inner beast, requiring Calvinistic vigilance. Marx had little sense of existence apart from abstract economic and social arrangement, a view from the air. The modern destruction of the planet reflects Plato's preference for an extraterrestrial, ideal:

> Large-scale technocratic industry concentrates power, alienates workers, unleashes ecological irresponsibility, and increases States' capacity for suicidal warfare without regard to whether production is ultimately controlled by corporate or State bureaucracies. Neither capitalism nor communism offers a proven alternative. One is ethnocidal in effect, and the other by design. (Barsh 208)

However, Marxism is not the first "great religion" to be "ethnocidal by design." Its intention to level national differences emulates the Christian effort to erase religious ones.

The central paradox in Neihardt's representation of Western thought combines the desire to unify humanity while separating it from lower forms of life, and in turn separating all forms of life from transcendental spirit. An article entitled "Black Elk's Platonism" by Daniel A. Dombrowski interestingly accentuates cultural differences by mistakenly attributing to Black Elk passages that were invented by Neihardt. With ironic consistency Black Elk's "Platonism" turns out to be exclusively Neihardt's. Following Eliade, following Jung, following Plato, Dombrowski defines Black Elk's reality as an imitation of an archetype that proves its own existence since Black Elk had no "direct contact" with Platonists. Neihardt, of course, believed in such contact whether direct or not: "Sometimes this close sense of the unity of all time and all human experience has come upon me so strongly that I have felt, for an intense moment, how just a little hurry on my part might get me there in time to hear . . . Socrates telling his dreams to his judges" (*The Song of Three Friends* viii, qtd. in Whitney 18).

From much the same belief in a universal mind, Neihardt felt that Black Elk's voice was somehow his own "as though I myself were telling the things he told me" (DeMallie, "Lakota Legacy" 114; see also *The Sixth Grandfather* 41). In a 1921 speech he sums up his belief in this imperative, collective need: "It must be made possible for the one to live vicariously the life of the many from the beginning" (Whitney 29). It is Neihardt, not Black Elk who conceives of the other world as both ideal and imminent in the proposed Lakota-Platonism Dombrowski quotes: "Crazy Horse dreamed and went into the world where there is nothing but the spirits of all things. That is the real world that is behind this one, and everything we see here is something like a shadow from that world" (*Black Elk Speaks* 85). Most of the material on Crazy Horse in *Black Elk Speaks* was derived from written sources (*The Sixth Grandfather* 51, 77), although this particular passage is largely Neihardt's invention. Neither the historical accounts nor Black Elk describe the spirit world as casting this kind of shadow on reality.

During the horse dance the Black Elk of *Black Elk Speaks* has a vision which lessens the importance of the ceremony except as it reveals (to Black Elk alone) the truly real: "I looked about me and could see that what we were doing was like a shadow cast upon the earth from yonder vision in the heavens, so bright it was and clear. I knew the real was yonder and the darkened dream of it was here" (*Black Elk Speaks* 169). Dombrowski's gloss asserts that this world is a shadow "because of the great brightness of 'that' one, as in Plato's myth of the sun in the Republic [Book VI]," where the Idea of the Good is the light source of human knowledge. Black Elk's actual statement in *The Sixth Grandfather* is not a humble recognition of human limits but an affirmation of the embodiment of spiritual power in the immediately present ceremony: "I looked at what I was doing and saw that I was making just exactly what I saw in the cloud. This on earth was like a shadow of that in the cloud. And then on behalf of my people I sent my voice to the spirits in the cloud like this, 'Hey-a-a-hey' (four times)" (*The Sixth Grand-father* 220).

Black Elk's shadow is like a natural shadow, accurately reflecting another form, not something lesser than the other form. That the Thunder beings have verified their alliance to the people through Black Elk's vision is a cause for rejoicing. The participants have achieved the Thunders' power by acting as they act. They are a Thunder being nation and Black Elk's wordless song is a call to friends rather than a supplication. To be a shadow of the spirits here is to act in their image, to perform the ceremony correctly, to be "making" real what has been seen, remembered, and imagined. Embodiment is the culmination of the spiritual process, just as it is for the creative process. Fulfillment occurs when spiritual power enters into physical form.

Yet centuries of distancing the good from physical expression not surprisingly cause Neihardt and the unsuspecting Dombrowski to read Black Elk's achievement of fullness as a recognition (in the midst of a joyful ceremony) that this world must never be too highly loved, even in contemplating the survival of one's children on its surface. While a Lakota holy man, like an Old Testament patriarch, is blessed if he can see more generations of healthy, culturally conscious children, Dombrowski unwittingly helps us to discover Neihardt's otherworldly emphasis by again attributing it to Black Elk. In *Black Elk Speaks*, Black Elk answers his own sad descriptions of square boxes replacing the hoop with typically Christian consolation: "But there is another world" (196). In *The Sixth Grandfather* it is Drinks Water, a nineteenth century holy man whom Black Elk recalls as speaking prophetically of the gray houses, along side of which the people "shall starve to death" (290). After making this prediction Drinks Water dies of grief.

Black Elk says nothing of a subsequent journey to a better world but uses the story to comment forcefully on his people's condition in this world: "The Long Knives [Americans] have woven the gray blanket over us and we are now prisoners of

war" (*The Sixth Grandfather* 290). The sadness is not for the
transience of mortal certainty but that the cultural powers embodied in Drinks Water have temporarily disappeared: "Drinks
Water had the ability to make everything nearly—he made
sugar, tobacco, matches and other things just by his words
alone. This is probably the only man who had the power direct
from the Great Spirit and this is why he was so powerful" (*The
Sixth Grandfather* 290). Yet Black Elk says that he himself had
power directly from the six grandfathers. Quite obviously the
length and intensity of his interviews with Neihardt belie any
suicidal impulses in Black Elk. The powers of Drinks Water live
again in Black Elk's words, despite the gray pall of Long Knife
domination.

The crushing weight of the Long Knives was ideological as
much as physical, and Neihardt's influence on Black Elk's expression was a result of collective thought habits that Neihardt
could not escape, whether or not he considered himself religiously conventional. In one of the most widely read and respected history of ideas volumes, *The Image of Man*, Herschel
Baker quotes Plato as a major source of Christian dualism: "In
this present life, I reckon that we make the nearest approach to
knowledge when we have the least possible intercourse or communion with the body, and are not surfeited with the bodily nature, but keep ourselves pure until the hour when God himself
is pleased to release us" (qtd. in Baker 47). Yet Baker himself
reinforces a twentieth-century dualism between spiritual and intellectual effort, just as Marxists do, but from his own perspective as an enlightened rationalist: "Religion formulates man's in-
capacity for rational explanation; it celebrates and ritualizes his
impotence . . . Philosophy . . . confronts the data of experience, examines them with ostensible objectivity, and attempts
to explain and systematize them" (Baker 110).

If Black Elk's representative thinking is not like Western Christianity, neither is it like Western rationalism. The Lakota are sufficiently free of such dualism that it is possible, as in the case with
Black Elk, to subscribe to several religions at once. As Sitting
Bull advised his people at the beginning of the reservation period: "When you find anything good in the white man's road,

pick it up but when you find something bad . . . leave it alone" (Vestal, *Sitting Bull* 256). Lakota adaptability was expressed in various apparent compromises, especially religious ones, but when Neihardt asked Black Elk why he became a Catholic in 1904, he answered simply, "my children had to live in this world" (*The Sixth Grandfather* 47).

For the sake of his descendants in this world, Black Elk, an entirely traditional warrior and healer for nearly half the years he would come to live, chose to assume the mantle of an other-worldly religion. Unlike the relatively balanced forces centering Lakota rites, a tone of desperation characterized Dionysian and Orphic ceremonies now thought to prefigure essential Christian metaphors. Whereas Black Elk's horse dance confirmed a covenant of kinship with supernatural powers, the Orphic ancestors of Christianity "substituted placation for confraternity with the gods . . . Their rituals symbolized purgation and the removal of natural evil" (Baker 113). Humankind's only hope in such a state of mind was to worship a mediator who would raise them from human pollution to become divine themselves. Black Elk's mediation, on the other hand, is more like that of the Hebrew prophets—to have a supernatural power take pity on him so that his people will flourish in the physical world, not rise above it. But when the two cultures met, the burden of centuries of Dionysian fear was too great to shed, even for a well meaning man like Neihardt.

His view of history in the epic poetry perfectly exemplifies Baker's summation of the Dionysian-Augustinian trap: "Given the transcendent and absolute goodness of God, and the potential goodness of all His creation, the world—wicked though it be—becomes the theatre wherein is enacted the majestic working out of God's purposes" (Baker 164). And Neihardt's view of humanity is unmistakably similar to Augustine's as well: "Adam was a kind of Platonic *eidos*—the Form of all humanity—and thus every man's share in Adam's sin became unarguable" (Baker 171). All people are therefore children of darkness, especially in *The Song of the Messiah,* until the light of Grace arrives and, in this sense of common descent from sinners, they come to share a kinship consisting primarily of their common

blindness. Only the extraordinary saint, as Neihardt considered
Black Elk, will, like the Hebrew Prophets, be chosen to be
dazzled by a light that even he can barely understand. Highly
ritualized religions have developed rigorous ways of maintain-
ing the spiritual awareness necessary for healing of every kind.
An Orphic religion is impatient with ritual, considering it a
brief exercise on the road to Damascus, an earthly obstruction
to clear progress toward the beyond. Even the eminent Christian rationalist Erasmus, could not abide the earthiness of ritual.
He wrote in order to correct "the common error of those who
make religion consist of ceremonies and an almost more than
Jewish observance of corporeal matters, while they are sin-
gularly careless of things that belong to piety" (letter, qtd. in
Baker 263).

Neihardt similarly had little patience for the religious practice
of conventional religion but preferred to marvel at mystical
dreams, especially his own call to become a poet when he was
eleven years old (*The Sixth Grandfather* 42). He saw Black Elk at
first in his own image, but while Neihardt resisted convention,
Lakota culture consistently channeled individual dreams into
religious forms that were basically but never exactly the same.
Neihardt values his dreams for their glimpses of a world per-
ceived only by a few. Black Elk felt his extraordinary vision
to be an obligation to serve the many and suffered from the burden of knowledge he could not distribute (*The Sixth Grandfather*
43, 57). For Neihardt, the limits of distribution only served
to divide an extremely small flock of sheep from a vast plain
of goats.

Neihardt's identity as a European and Christian thinker must
be reiterated to counterbalance the assumption of his being
Lakota by special sympathy. In addition to the Neihardt who
read almost no contemporary literature (Whitney 18), the Neihardt who rode the crest of Manifest Destiny should not be forgotten. American expansion made Platonic dualism into a the-
atrical allegory. As Roy Harvey Pearce has said in the classic
account of how whites drew upon their cultural traditions to jus-
tify conquest: "American Indians were everywhere found to be,
simply enough, men who were not men, who were religiously

and politically incomplete" (Pearce 6). The incompleteness was considered by more benevolent observers such as Neihardt, to be remediable in God's good time and with the help of his appointed messengers. Indians were (and still are) equated by missionaries with the Jews who will eventually be guided to the true faith: "Americans . . . would have to be loving and patient with these poor ignorant wandering Israelites" (Pearce 62; see also 46). In 1824 William H. Keaton wrote of his travels in Illinois in such a way as to foreshadow Neihardt's romanticizing of Black Elk. His Indians proved that they had seeds "implanted by the Great Creator himself; that civilization does not produce them; that the real benefit which results from [civilization] is, that, in some instances, it may curb the passions which would otherwise impede their growth" (qtd. in Pearce 108).

Nevertheless, Lewis Henry Morgan wrote that the Iroquois lacked the "progressive spirit," being content to monotonously repeat the same activities, stubbornly (like the Jews) preserving old forms and old customs. Seeing Black Elk's people through the same assumptions, Neihardt overlooks the narrative sophistication of Black Elk's words: "If it were literature instead of dance ritual, it would be a literary masterpiece," he wrote to a friend (DeMallie, "Lakota Legacy" 124). Even though the vision becomes the horse dance, Neihardt seems to forget that he has experienced neither vision nor dance but only Black Elk's verbal art. Ingrained concepts of progress allow him to assert that Indian cultures "did not develop beyond the dance and the litigation" (1931 letter qtd. in Holler, "Lakota Religion" 30). But if Neihardt believed in the dead-endedness of Indian culture, he was at least in prestigious company. No less an appreciator of the natural than Thoreau felt compelled to admit: "The fact is, the history of the white man is a history of improvement, that of the red man a history of fixed habits of stagnation" (Thoreau, XVI, 251–52, qtd. in Pearce 149).

Yet, Thoreau, like Neihardt wished to give the savages their due by assigning them their usual portion of innate nobility: "The thought of a so-called savage tribe is generally far more just than that of a single civilized man" (Thoreau I, 52–53, qtd. in Pearce 150). Predictably Indians, if they are admired at all, have more heart than head. In *Hiawatha,* for generations the major image of Indians to most Americans, "There are longings, yearnings, strivings/ For the good they comprehend not" (qtd. in Pearce 192). Therefore an Indian consciousness "existed . . . for white men to outgrow" (Pearce 195). But in the view of benevolent Christians from William Penn (Pearce 35–38) to William Stolzman, the contemporary Jesuit author of *The Pipe and Christ,* Indians are preordained to serve as examples for both whites and Christian Indians of universal conversion, God's unfolding love for all mankind.

The harsher view of Indian backwardness cannot be ascribed to liberals like Neihardt or Stolzmann. For them, those who are backward will soon come forward. For John Adams, on the other hand, the Indians were too "bigoted in their religion" to ever be converted, and their religion is to blame for their "invincible aversion both to civilization and Christianity" (qtd. in Drinnon 77). Just as zealous, but characteristically more attentive to the means of solving the problem rather than simply castigating its source, Benjamin Franklin recommended a technology for conquest and genocide: "If it be the design of Providence to extirpate these savages in order to make room for the cultivators of the earth, it seems not improbable that rum may be the appointed means" (qtd. in Drinnon 100). This is a cruder statement of the American desire to have Indians actually vanish than the coaxing of Indians into assimilative salvation. Both beliefs, however, agree to the unquestioning inferiority of Native American culture.

Many Americans believed Indians to be "demoniac" worshippers of the devil, while others considered them to be inferior to Christians only in not yet having received the full light of scripture. Few to this day consider Native American culture to be as advanced as their own. Neihardt may not have considered Lakota culture to be capable of literature, but he did not view Indians as racially inferior in the sense that believers in Manifest Destiny justified their brutality. According to President John Quincy Adams, Secretary of State, Henry Clay, informed an 1825 cabinet meeting "that it was impossible to civilize Indians, that there never was a full-blooded Indian who took to civilization. It was not in their nature. He [Clay] believed they were destined to extinction, and, although he would never use or countenance inhumanity towards them, he did not think them, as a race, worth preserving" (Adams, qtd. in Drinnon 179).

Gradations of racism are distinct in a nineteenth century context. Mark Twain's patronizing conception of blacks is not as vicious as Clay's *de facto* genocide, while Neihardt's Indian characters have more variety and humanity than Twain's blacks. Neihardt's God creates no inferior races, only separate cultures coming to the light at rates appropriate to their created traits. Indians, he implies, are still children, but only because God has determined their rate of growth to be slower than that of whites for the ultimate edification of all. Neihardt is one of the clearest, ablest proponents of this view, which is best understood in a detailed reading of his works. There it can be seen that Neihardt's view of "Aryan" character implied superiority but, like Mark Twain's, was consciously intended to show only difference. The Aryan statement is racist but not psychotically so in the manner of General Sherman writing to President Grant in 1866: "We must act with vindictive earnestness against the Sioux, even to their extermination, men, women, and children. Nothing else will reach the root of this case" (qtd. in Drinnon 329). Although Sherman was reacting to a military defeat (the Fetterman fight of December 21, 1866), few generals of his day would have responded to a European enemy by an all-out attack on noncombatants, if only because a white enemy was human and would be dealt with by the rules of civilized warfare.

Indian warfare, on the other hand, served the psychological purpose of repressing vulnerability of any kind. John Adams, Benjamin Franklin, Henry Clay, William Tecumseh Sherman, coalesced in Theodore Roosevelt at the end of the century extolling the reign of the fittest: "That the barbarians recede or are conquered . . . is due solely to the power of the mighty civilized races which have not lost the fighting instinct, and which by their expansion are gradually bringing peace into the red wastes where the barbarian peoples of the word hold sway" (from *The Strenuous Life,* qtd. in Drinnon 232). Drinnon goes on to show how Indian hating and Indian fighting became Asian hating and fighting in subsequent generations. These examples of extreme American racism make it easier for us to describe Neihardt fairly without being constrained to simply reverse the eulogizing. The context should also make it easier to understand Black Elk in relation to a more plausible Neihardt, rather than simply as a story of mutual mysticism or, conversely, as a translation from which the original voices have vanished.

THREE

Neihardt's Christian Matrix

L<small>IKE</small> Neihardt but over fifty years later, William Stolzman, S. J. gained the confidence of several of the most respected
wicaśa wakan on the Rosebud and Pine Ridge reservations. Stolzman learned the Lakota language, participated in the vision
quest, and organized a series of meetings between himself and
the medicine men at which the religions were comparatively
discussed. Unlike most missionaries before him but like Neihardt, Stolzman had mysterious personal experiences and believes that the Lakota ceremonies are an overture to experienc-
ing a valid supernatural reality (Stolzman 211–14). Neihardt
metaphorically compares Lakota religion to Christianity, while
Stolzman compares the religions analytically and systematically.
The Pipe and Christ is a detailed discussion of the most important Lakota beliefs and ceremonies, sequentially followed by descriptions of Catholic analogues.

The book is thorough, clear, and precise, especially in its
descriptions of contemporary Lakota ritual. As might be expected, however, Stolzman describes this representatively pre-
Christian revelation as a limited truth soon to be transcended by
the Church's more mature creed. Stolzman's position is virtually
the same as Neihardt's in *The Song of the Messiah,* or even Milton's
in *Samson Agonistes,* but it is conveyed in practical, persuasive
prose. A major distinction, emphasized throughout *The Pipe and
Christ* and centuries of Christian thought, asserts that the Lakota
religion like Judaism and other "primitive" religions "are very
concerned with physical health while Christian spirituality is
more concerned about the health of one's soul" (Stolzman 215).

This is phrased as if to give equal weight to both concerns, but Stolzman concludes his book with a Christianity-or-else admonition. The Lakota religion is to be practiced "for the life and health of the Lakota people," while the Christian religion provides the "context" of the universal need for "eternal salvation" (218).

The latter concern is so urgent that the Lakota religion can be important only as it is conducive to making its adherents receptive to the Word. Lakota spiritual beliefs and rituals are like the Jewish religion, materialistic and tribal, but they both prepare the way for the ultimately universal "coming of Christ, the Messiah and Son of God" (211). This gradual, unequal rate of conversion is "providential," though "Christian revelation and rituals are always subsequent and more universal" (212). That the Lakota are a specially favored people is attested to by the statement that "almost the entire Lakota people was converted to Christianity within a generation after they came on the reservation" (211). Though he mentions that the Jews were specially prepared for Christ's coming, Stolzman implies that the Lakotas' prior conversion shows that they may consider themselves a chosen people. Stolzman draws upon another key missionary doctrine to assure contemporary Lakota that their ancestors who were ignorant of Christianity were nevertheless saved. Their benighted religious practices rendered them "Religiously Natural Christians" (39).

It is obviously another matter and another fate, however, for those who knowing Christ refused to emerge from the darkness. Stolzman tells the Lakota that they must not follow the foolish refusal of the Jews, who do not accept Christ as the Messiah because

> they have great difficulty spiritualizing their world view to see that the Kingdom of God is not ultimately a kingdom of this material earth but a transformed Kingdom of heaven on earth in Christ Jesus. Nonetheless, by his blood and birth, Jesus has a special, personal association with all the Jewish people, who to this day are bearers of the promise. One might call them "invited Christians". (Stolzman 40)

The Lakota too are invited to shed their crude materiality. Why should they consider the *hunka* (making of relatives) ceremony to be a legitimate sanctification of relationship when they can undergo baptism? "While the strengthening of the individual in baptism primarily takes place through the internalized action of Christ's Spirit, the strengthening of the individual in the *hunkayapi* [they are relatives] ceremony is external to the *hunka* [participant] through the material and physical actions of the new relatives" (31). Why should the Lakota adhere to a tribal clannishness when they can partake of "the universal unity under the descendant of Peter, whom Christ appointed as the rock on which he would build his Church and to whom he gave the 'keys' to the Kingdom" (42)? And why should the Lakota sitting in the sweat lodge plead for help from external spirits when the Kingdom is within the Church and within the person? It is grossly demonstrative to take off one's clothes before entering the sweat lodge to *show* humility, unlike entering "the confessional weak, sinful, and alone with humility and hope" (52), having internalized expression in the soul, abandoning physical display.

Avoiding the counterproductive impact of condemning the central ceremony in the Lakota tradition, the sun dance, Stolzman implies that the Lakota will follow and pass beyond the experience of the Jews who abandoned bodily sacrifice: "God moved Judeo-Christian people away from physical sacrifices of animals and flesh to the sacrifice of one's spirit" (77). Enlightened people realize that Christian sacrifice absolves them of sacrificing animals (as in the *heyoka* feast, *The Sixth Grandfather* 232–35) or undergoing the physical rigor of fasting, piercing, and flesh offerings. Attention should be directed away from the body's health and toward the transformation of the spirit.

In addition to showing the limitations of dwelling only in the body, Stolzman undidactically instructs the Lakota to transcend their tribalism and clannishness by giving themselves fully to participation in a universal family of saved souls. As usual the Lakota are given a choice between being like the parochial Jews in concentrating only on their immediate tribal welfare and future earthly survival, or becoming dedicated to joining the souls of all saved human beings in heaven:

> In the Old Testament God identified Israel as "his son," and the commendments related offenses against other Israelites with offenses against God. In the New Testament the Son of God is identified with the Son of Man; the incarnation unites the divine and human orders of things and makes violations against other Christians and other humans into violations against Christ and his Father. (72)

Tribalism and therefore the need for tribal religions, as Stolzman implies but cleverly does not state, have been superseded by a covenant or kinship alliance that is obviously superior in a moral and practical sense. If you do not accept it, your sins will not be washed away and you will die believing in a broken treaty:

> The sacrifice of the lamb is associated with the Jews' deliverance from the hand of the Angel of Death and slavery of Pharaoh. It was the sign of the Jewish Passover and covenant with the Lord in the Old Testament and a sign of the new covenant achieved through the sacrifice of Jesus, the Lamb of God who takes away the sins of the world. (161)

Knowing the emotional depth of the word *oyate* (the people) in Lakota prayers, Stolzman works steadily in his book to change the concept of the people's immortality on earth, as the central object of work and prayer, to a meditation on Christ as the active savior of a humanity whose individual members survive in Eternity. While the Jews emphasized the transmission of their cultural consciousness from father to son, "Christ went beyond this . . . it was not the Jewish people but himself that was the bearer of the promise and inheritance of God's people . . . God's people would come to share not so much an earthly kingdom but a heavenly one" (186). Statements like this are so heavily weighted as to virtually erase not only the extensive descriptions of Lakota ceremonies, but even Stolzman's own stated belief in the existence of Lakota spirits throughout the book. He explains the explicit description of his vision quest, usually not revealed in a public forum (see Amiotte, "Eagles Fly Over" 28, 37), as intended to "lift the spiritual hopes, dreams, and faith of the people" (2). Perhaps he means "lift" to the level of Christianity.

In the tradition of Christian thought that formed the mind of Neihardt and still shapes the work and expression of Christians concerned with augmenting lesser lights, Stolzman consistently allows non-Christians to retain a sense of being favored by God but with a revelation that God for his own mysterious purposes wished to have gradually diffused. "It is commonly recognized that the study of comparative religions deepens an appreciation for one's own religion, and fosters a great respect and theological acceptance of others" (67). During his vision quest, Stolzman experienced unusual shifts in the winds, heard the scream of the Thunder bird, heard the innumerable voices of the Lakota dead, felt a small earthquake as a sign of comfort from Grandmother earth, and observed supernatural changes in the moon and stars. His description is more than respectful since he considers the miracles to have come directly from God.

Like Neihardt, Stolzman believes the Lakota have a special gift of communicating with higher forms of being. The Lakota spirits are benevolent and when Stolzman asks them through a medicine man if they "know Jesus Christ," he is stunned by the succinct profundity of their answer: *"mahpiya ekta na maka śitomni"* 'into heaven and throughout the earth' (125). Stolzman interprets this as expressing the "Ascension of Christ into heaven and his glorification there as God, far above the stars of the Lakota spirits" (125). But the words may mean only that the concept of Jesus emphasizes transcendence of the earth and universal belief. "Ekta" means *toward* the sky, not into heaven. In a basic interpretive sense, Stolzman is overreading the material when he rhapsodizes, *"mahpiya ekta* says much more than Jesus is divine. It speaks of his being transcendentalized into God's glory from the world below" (125). Then he seals one mysteriously suggestive revelation with the proclaimed weight of centuries-old dogma: "Christ's Spirit is no better than all the other Lakota spirits who know and help the people concretely in this world. The coupling of these two phrases together says, at least to me, 'Jesus is above us in one area, but he's just like us in another'" (126). The righteous pagan is once again enlightened with the reassurance that God loved them before and still loves them by revealing a higher aspect of themselves.

Despite his many accurate descriptions and actual participation in Lakota religion, Stolzman betrays a cultural arrogance he is unable to transcend. The Lakota ceremonies by his own accounts are long and detailed, yet Stolzman's summation of their complexity is contradictory and demeaning: "Pre-Christian revelations still have unique spiritual powers to sanctify our religious reality on the most fundamental levels. It is like the person who studying calculus realizes that one must study and understand more deeply the fundamentals of arithmetic" (67). His comparative metaphors are only backhanded compliments, sometimes absurdly so: The Lakota religion is like a hand, "natural and close to the things of the world," while the Christian religion is like a glove which can "do things a bare hand cannot do" (209). The glove is capable of effecting supernatural deeds.

Another "fit" metaphor suits Stolzman's stance of respect even less. The Lakota religion is like a horse, "feeding off the earth." The Christian religion is like a wagon, and Jesus is the driver: "While a person does not try to put the glove in the hand or the wagon in the horse, he may put the hand in the glove and the horse between the poles of a wagon" (210). Stolzman's second metaphor has a certain historical irony in that he connects "superior" technology to true religion, but there is no irony in his final classification of the culture he pretends to objectively describe in order to establish mutual respect: "while the Christian religion welcomes pre-Christian enrichments, the Lakota religion does not welcome them. Why this is so will become clearer when we consider the difference between second-level, national, folk religions and third level, international, cosmopolitan religions" (210).

Why should some stiffnecked non-Christians resist conversion? Stolzman patiently forgives them for not seeing the embracing comprehensiveness of the Church. Eventually both religions will exist with equal validity, one as first grade arithmetic, the second as pure calculus. In the meantime children must be brought along gently. The Jewish and Lakota religions are a wholesome Sesame Street. But when their child-like believers reach adolescence, Catholic priests can best initiate them to spiritual adulthood. William K. Powers has pointed out that priests who use a pipe in the mass and whose vestments are ornamented with beads and quills intend to help those who already believe in the pipe progress to a belief in Christ:

> would we ever be willing to admit that the priest believed in the efficacy of the pipe? Were the trappings of native religion now part of his religious system? . . . We . . . accept the priestly overtures as a strategem of the Catholic church, which, in the words of the Jesuits, "uses the best of any culture for its own advantage." (*Beyond the Vision* 99)

The conviction of Christian religious superiority is evident throughout the English language literature in which the ambitious epic poet, John Neihardt, was educated. Ironically, some Jesuit missionaries accused Neihardt of bribing and flattering Black Elk into pretending to a tradition he had long discarded. Carl J. Starkloff, S. J. writes that Neihardt deliberately passed over

> the fact that Black Elk, the Lakota medicine man, was also Nicolaus Black Elk after his conversion to Catholicism in the early years of this century, and that as Nicolaus Black Elk he served as a catechist on the Pine Ridge Reservation for many years. Perhaps as a poet Neihardt was also a bit of a primitivist and a romantic. (Starkloff 159–60)

Starkloff and Joseph Zimmerman S. J. who oversaw Black Elk's written recantation of his *Black Elk Speaks* heresy (*The Sixth Grandfather* 59), apparently missed Neihardt's almost heavy-handed urging of a doctrine of spiritual evolution in harmony with their own.

Neihardt was a self-professed man of letters. His education would almost certainly have included the English and American authors most widely accepted as major, and as models for serious poetry. Many of those same writers in turn derive their most emphatic metaphors from the King James Bible and their visions of the world from a surprisingly limited number of interpretations of that Bible. As an artist, Neihardt was a descendant of such thoroughly Christian writers as John Milton and Nathaniel Hawthorne. Certainly Neihardt would have attended to Milton as the greatest writer of epic poetry in the English language, the one to emulate in his own *Song of the Indian Wars* and *Song of the Messiah*. And though they are far from being poets, the Jesuit writers Stolzman and Starkloff share the common vision which determined relationships between Europeans and Indians from the beginning.

Throughout the middle ages, Renaissance, and into the nineteenth century, non-Christians have been literarily exploited to prove the superiority of Western religion and culture as well as the innate intelligence and finer sensibilities of those Neihardt termed "Aryans." In 1583, Sir George Peckham, an English Catholic nobleman, wishing to establish a New England haven for English Catholics, theorized that the Indians would freely offer "all the commodities they can yeelde up" in exchange for being led "from superstitious idolatrie to sincere Christianity, from the divell to Christ, from hell to heaven" (qtd. in Cave 282). While conversionary zeal was too often a shallow rationalization of this sort, the New England Puritans intently held to the gradual, providentially guided illumination expressed, though not so peacefully awaited, by Fathers Starkloff and Stolzman. They expected "God's Elect would of their own accord emulate the English." Unfortunately "vengeance against the heathen" soon took precedence over a less expedient hope (Cave 291).

Perhaps the most charitable view of heathen virtue taken by an early Puritan was that of Milton in his classically modeled verse tragedy, *Samson Agonistes*. The play explains why God does not make everyone Christian from the beginning. Pagans are the tragic heroes who struggle toward the light without consciously knowing it in their physical lifetimes, so that the audience of Christian witnesses may know the full range of spirituality, from fear and anxiety through anger and a refusal to accept God's creation, to a final recogition of ultimate bliss, the heavenly rose encircling the cross. In his first speech Samson asks why he has been given such great earthly strength if he "must die/ Betrayed, captivated, and both my eyes put out" (ll. 32–33). The play asserts the usual pattern; the eyes of physical and natural pride must be put out; man's lesser self must be crucified so that salvation which is reception of the Word, the truth, may be "accomplished" (John 20:28). God loves man despite his sin, despite the Fall, despite his innate blindness. Samson's strength cannot bring down the Philistine temple of delusory pride; only God could inexplicably and gloriously release men from suffering and blindness into heaven, which is blissfully instantaneous metaphysical recognition. Acting as the Chorus, Manoa, Samson's father, concludes the play: "All is is best, though we oft doubt/ What th' unsearchable dispose/ Of Highest Wisdom brings about,/ And ever best found in the close" (ll. 1745–58).

Neihardt's oft-repeated crucifixion imagery, used to describe the carnage at Wounded Knee, bears the same obvious intent of purging pity or vengefulness by making the event a revelation foreshadowing Judgment Day, ushering in a full and universal comprehension of the Word. Milton, and Neihardt after him, do not believe that saving enlightenment can be achieved by man's own efforts. It is always a gift conferred inexplicably without regard for good works or earthly virtue. Calvin is the most notable exponent of salvation as mystery rather than reward, as explained by Roland Mushat Frye:

> Man's "total depravity," then, emphatically did not imply that he was totally evil in a temporal sense; it only meant that in all its parts (hence "totally") man's nature was so marred by sin that he could not at any point in his life act so purely as to merit God's grace and the life everlasting. (Frye 106)

Pre-Christian Jews, Greeks, or Indians were not morally inferior, ony temporarily positioned in more darkness than light. Richard Hooker staunchly defended these lesser lights as nevertheless revealing a modicum of truth "to detract from the dignity thereof were to injury even God himself, who being that light which none can approach unto, hath sent out these lights whereof we are capable, even as so many sparkles resembling the bright fountain from which they rise" (qtd. in Fry 87).

The metaphor of God as a vast light, covered by slowly shrinking pockets of darkness, is one of Neihardt's most frequently used biblical symbols. Catholic philosophers of the Renaissance such as Erasmus confirmed the view carried on by missionaries like Stolzman, that God intended a partial revelation of the truth, giving some portion of the light to each nation, even to each individual. The unification of the separate lights is the eternal daylight of eternity that can be glimpsed in brief God-sent dreams, visions, or inspired fiction. Neihardt emphasized this metaphor as thoroughly as Hawthorne did in *The Scarlet Letter,* either because he may have read that work and consciously or unconsciously emulated it, or because the metaphor of light may be the most widely used physical image of God in the Christian tradition. But Hawthorne and Neihardt use light especially as a means of unifying separate members of the human family. Their works are flashes of light in the darkness, meteors to augur the second coming.

Light coming through darkness suffuses the whole text of *The Scarlet Letter,* but the scene most appropriate for comparison to Neihardt occurs in chapter 12, "The Minister's Vigil." As an erring soul rather than a tragic hero (in a hypothetical Christian interpretation), Arthur Dimmesdale refuses to acknowledge his responsibilities to his family and to God. He is the father of Hester Prynne's child, and in not wholeheartedly embracing their common purpose of assisting God's creation, he has sacrificed the greatest human gift, the "Pearl" of great price. Weakened by guilt, frozen in egoic fear, he stands on the scaffold where Hester stood, in the darkness of midnight, as if to condemn and redeem himself. Even in his debilitated state (original sin), he has a great vision, which like Black Elk he is initially too immature to understand. All the people of the town, he vividly imagines, will emerge into the new day to see their sainted minister on the scaffold of shame.

Just then, Hester and Pearl, returning from Governor Winthrop's death bed (the symbolic death of pride), see him and join him on the scaffold. In a typological foreshadowing of the new life that awaits all fallen individuals in the recognition of God's universal compassion, the minister feels "a tumultuous rush of new life, other life than his own, pouring like a torrent into his heart and hurrying through all his veins, as if the mother and the child were communicating their vital warmth to his half-torpid system. The three formed an electric chain" (Hawthorne 148). But when Pearl asks if the minister will stand with them "tomorrow noontide" in this manner, Dimmesdale cannot yet take up his cross: "'At the great judgment day,' whispered the minister—and, strangely enough, the sense that he was a professional teacher of the truth impelled him to answer the child so" (149).

And just so Neihardt concludes his *Song of the Messiah*. The injustice done to the American Indians is like the suffering of Samson and of Dimmesdale. Christian "readers" of reality will benefit by learning to endure the predestined darkness. Injustice is done as long as the earth lasts, but love is simultaneously revealed in different degrees to each reader of the cosmic story. Neihardt highlights an extraordinary meteor, which appears after Sitting Bull's death, for the same theologically thematic reason that brings a meteor into *The Scarlet Letter*'s central chapter. Immediately after Dimmesdale says that the human family will not be revealed as one, a meteor promises that the revelation is assuredly continual until it becomes constant. In the ordinary, spiritually invisible scene of street and houses, the eye suddenly sees all the signs of entry into the life to come, including the road to reach it:

> the doorsteps and thresholds, with the early grass springing up about them; the garden plots, black with freshly turned earth; the wheel-track, little worn, and even in the market place, margined with green on either side—all were visible, but with a singularity of aspect that seemed to give another moral interpretation to the things of this world than they had ever borne before. (Hawthorne 149)

Hester, Pearl, and Arthur "stood in the noon of that strange and solemn splendor as if it were the light that is to reveal all secrets and the daybreak that shall unite all who belong to one another" (Hawthorne 149–50).

One of Neihardt's favorite words for Indian understanding in his poetry is "dim." Perhaps Hawthorne similarly names his protagonist "Dimmesdale," as if to suggest the limits of wisdom in the shadows of the earth. While Hawthorne and Neihardt intend the discerning reader to understand the unifying purpose in God's "book" of Creation as the Renaissance theologians called it, pagans like King Lear and Julius Caesar are tragically deceived by the light of dimmer stars, impaired cultural perspectives. Hawthorne's narrator describes how the Puritan people of New England were obsessed only with the welfare of their own nation, a version of the narrow tribalism attributed by Stolzman to the Lakota:

> a blazing spear, a sword of flame, a bow, or a sheaf of arrows, seen in the midnight sky, prefigured Indian warfare . . . We doubt whether any marked event, for good or evil, ever befell New England, from its settlement down to Revolutionary times, of which the inhabitants had not been previously warned by some spectacle of this nature . . . their infant commonwealth was under a celestial guardianship of peculiar intimacy and strictness. (Hawthorne 150)

The limitation of "chosen" pride is complemented by the even greater limitation of Dimmesdale who thinks the Heavens have spoken not just to his colony but to him alone. The universalism of Christ's message, as promulgated by Paul, is stressed by one noted American writer recollecting his own "primitive" forbears and by another less noted one describing the tragedy of a transitional cult, the Ghost Dance religion, advancing toward heaven but still having to suffer the ordained darkness of unequal race and nationhood:

> lie not one to another, seeing that ye have put off the old man with his deeds; And have put on the new man, which is renewed in knowledge after the image of him that created him: Where there is neither Greek nor Jew, circumcision, or uncircumcision, Barbarian, Scythian, bond nor free; but Christ is all, and in all. (Colossians 3:9–11)

FOUR

Neihardt's Mission
and Black Elk's Center

PUBLISHED five years after *Black Elk Speaks, The Song of
the Messiah* was Neihardt's favorite work, one that the interviews with Black Elk only served to deepen and foreshadow. It
has been laudatorily interpreted by Raymond J. DeMallie, who
concentrates on Sitanka (Big Foot), Neihardt's hero, martyred
at Wounded Knee. In recognizing the soldier who kills him as
his brother, Sitanka (and Neihardt) "overcomes the petty differences that separate Indians from whites" and achieves "mystical
recognition of the power of the common human spirit," also
a "synthesis of the message of *Black Elk Speaks*" (DeMallie,
"Lakota Legacy" 126). Both works, according to DeMallie,
elicit pity and the comforting thought that "each of us is only
human, pathetically manipulating our lives, unable to understand the simplest truths that both underlie and obviate our
struggles" ("Lakota Legacy" 126).

Such collective self-pity is in keeping with neither Black Elk's
Lakota perception of suffering nor with Neihardt's Christian
one. Neihardt's portrayals of the Ghost Dance and especially of
Wounded Knee are persuasively Christian. The Ghost Dance
approaches but does not quite reach Neihardt's own advanced
faith because it separates Indians from whites in its eschatological
promise, although it unites the tribes in a pantribal spiritual alliance more powerful than any in history, including that of
Tecumseh. The *Song* celebrates this approach to God's love
through a new revelation, significantly more mature than the

traditional religions such as that recited in *Black Elk Speaks*. Neihardt apparently derived enough from Black Elk to stimulate his perception of American Indians providentially emerging into the light in his time and partly through his own efforts.

The end of the Indian culture at Wounded Knee is as far from sad as the death of Samson in *Samson Agonistes*. Neihardt is Big Foot's Manoa. But just as Samson, like surviving heroes of explicitly Western literature is a type or prefiguration of Christ, so Big Foot and the Lakota people are precursors of Christian salvation, which must of mythological necessity be preceded by a crucifixion. Neihardt's metaphors are heavy-handed statements of his purpose, which is more specifically devotional than aesthetic or, as DeMallie has it, "humanistic." The passage from Colossians quoted above, refers to people unified in belief and in the assurance of salvation, not in a bond of common humanity, per se.

Neihardt is an apostolic poet, intending to make the Word, as verbal incarnation of God, redemptive for his readers. Sequentially reflecting this process, Big Foot's achievement of Christlike forgiveness is gradually revealed. Mankind's greatest blessing is to receive the Word, the true message and being of God, in a mediating form, the body of Christ, or works of mystically inspired language. Humanity's greatest suffering occurs when the Word's power to lovingly unify is temporarily obscured. When people forget their union with their kin in Christian fellowship, their inhumanity assumes its demonic play. All human suffering is a crucifixion carried on by those who do not recognize their fellows as themselves and the divine spirit in all things. God allows the darkness in his wisdom so that the light can be gradually displayed, so that the story of crucifixion and redemption can sufficiently amplify and universalize itself until Judgment Day. The Lakota suffer at Wounded Knee as Christ suffered on the cross, so that a lesser understanding can be transformed to unifying love.

The Hotchkiss guns begin the sound that is gradually modulated to the redemptive gospel, in the same way that Christ's suffering on the cross is inseparable from his eventual ascendance into heaven: "And then—as though the whole world, crucified / Upon the heaped Golgotha of its years, / For all its lonely silences of tears, / Its countless hates and hurts and terrors, found / A last composite voice—a hell of sound / Assailed the brooding heavens" (Neihardt, *The Song of the Messiah* 108). As Satan assailed God, so all human violence is a rebellion against accepting spiritual equality in the common fatherhood of God. And as Christ saw his father in the midst of his suffering, Big Foot sees God and hears him even in the unrevealing soul of his enemy. Evil is primarily the inability to see and articulate unity for Neihardt: "A soldier's face with haggard eyes that blazed, / A wry wound of a mouth agape to shout, / And nothing but the silence coming out / An agony of silence. For a span, / Unmeasured as the tragedy of man" (*Messiah* 109). Christ's wounds represent a silence that produces words of love by evoking feelings of compassion.

This is the providential purpose of American Indian suffering, according to Neihardt. Wounded Knee is the hill of Calvary, the writhing body of Christ, but the souls of the people will escape all pain and suffering "Along the gully winding to the sky / The roaring followed, till the long, thin cry / Above it ceased" (*Messiah* 110). The poem ends with a promise of salvation, not salvation itself. After all, life on earth allows only momentary intimations of the truth, like that granted to Big Foot at the moment of death. DeMallie confuses the Lakota symbolism of snow as a "cleansing" expression of the northern spirits with Neihardt's use of the blizzard metaphor at the end of the poem: "All night it swept / The bloody field of victory that kept / The secret of the Everlasting Word" (*Messiah* 110). The blizzard returns the reader to the obscurity of the fallen world where the Everlasting Word must be treasured as a memory and a promise. The blizzard disguises Love, like the bullets of the Seventh Cavalry. The poem, like the devotional literature on which it is based, must relinquish the reader to the earthly world in which the truth is covered, but in the experience of reading, they will have learned to direct their yearning consciously toward the light.

The rest of *The Song of the Messiah* tells of the unconscious tropism which Christians have long observed in pagan peoples. Although Neihardt purportedly based his account of the Ghost Dance on Indian witnesses, much of the factual material is re-written from James Mooney's *The Ghost Dance Religion* (1896). And while he listened to elders like Black Elk and Standing Bear, Neihardt interpreted them according to Mooney and in emulative response to Christian literature. Mooney forthrightly praises Wovoka, the Messiah, by quoting an unnamed but "careful and competent" investigator: "He has given these people a better religion than they ever had before, taught them precepts which, if faithfully carried out, will bring them into better accord with their white neighbors, and has prepared the way for their final Christianization" (Mooney 25).

This goal is consistently expressed by Neihardt as the reception of the Word (the incarnate Christ), and in the third stanza of the poem, he expresses the poem's fulfillment in the metaphor of a late March night "When you could feel things waking underground / And all the world turned spirit, and you heard / Still thunders of the everlasting Word" (*Messiah* 2). Sound, throughout the poem, reflexively incarnates redemptive truth. The poem begins with faint echoes of that sound to keynote the power of the Ghost Dance religion and ends with the crucifying thunder of bullets to predict ultimate harmony.

In Section II, "The Coming of the Word," the visionary report of Good Thunder personifies the idealized pagan's pre-figuration of Christ, a more resonant promise than Black Elk's less Christianized symbols:

> And now, behold! a man was standing there
> Beneath the tree, his body painted red,
> A single eagle feather on his head,
> His arms held wide . . .
> A wound upon his side began to glow
> With many colors . . .
> Softly crooned
> The Tree, for now the colors of the wound

Became a still white happiness that spread
and filled the world of branches overhead
With blossom and the murmuring of birds. (*Messiah* 25–27)

Sound and light converge to bring beatitude to a crude and war-like people:

> Only those who have known the deadly hatred that once animated Ute, Cheyenne, and Pawnee, one toward another, and are able to contrast it with their present spirit of mutual brotherly love, can know what the Ghost-dance religion has accomplished in bringing the savage into civilization. It is such a revolution as comes but once in the life of a race. (Mooney 25)

While Good Thunder represents the most advanced of souls in his vision of cosmic charity (*Messiah* 17–28), the unreadiness of the Sioux as a people to reach heaven while still on earth only echoes similar unreadiness among the whites. Thus Kicking Bear's report of Wovoka's wonders, unlike that of Good Thunder, can only regress to emphasizing the Savior's punishment of sin: "And I have seen the greedy, faithless race / Before the waking fury of His face / Become a dream forgotten in the day" (*Messiah* 33). Dwelling more on the punishment of sinners, Kicking Bear cannot advance to the love and forgiveness embodied in Good Thunder and ultimately in Big Foot.

The darker, regressive forces among the Lakota are represented by the charlatan, Short Bull, and the romantically satanic Sitting Bull. Short Bull represents those who make gods of themselves, promising more than they can possibly deliver and thereby compounding the suffering they egocentrically exploit: "Or had the weed of self in some vain dream / Grown mightily, till everything was small / Save him, and in the glory of it all / He towered now?" (*Messiah* 64–65). Sitting Bull is meant to evoke more sympathy, since he conforms to the romanticized archetype of Satan. He represents the inevitable death of pagan religion as well as the transience of pride in the advancing soul of the beholder.

He is first represented as feeling the same despair Neihardt had attributed to Black Elk. In response to a warning that he should escape from the death rumored to be planned for him by the Indian agent, Sitting Bull is as stoic as Julius Caesar preparing to leave for the senate. But Sitting Bull's stoicism comes primarily from despair: "'I do not know,'/ Said Sitting Bull, and gazed upon the wall / With eyes that saw not anything at all / But lonely distance that is not of space" (73). Neihardt's Hunkpapa leader has gone beyond the righteous anger and excoriation of the white man's hypocrisy for which popular newspaper accounts had made him famous (Graham 65–73). He expresses his contempt for the *wašicu*'s world but only retrospectively. The earth has been

> stricken with a curse
> Of fools, who build their lodges up so high
> They lose their mother, and the father sky
> Is hidden in the darkness that they build;
> And with their traders' babble they have killed
> The ancient voices that could make them wise.
> Their mightiest in trickery and lies
> Are chiefs among them. (78)

Sitting Bull has lost the will to fight, perhaps as part of the general progression toward victory in Christian submission, as Neihardt sees the final triumph of the Sioux. In his death, however, he fails to achieve martyrdom, enticed backward into combat by a voice not unlike that of Lady Macbeth. As the Indian police are arresting him, the voice seduces him into resistance just as Short Bull falsely exalted his power to create invulnerability, or as any voice that rebelled against the United States or its God. The voice of the prior warlike culture haunts Sitting Bull as

> from the doorway followed, like a song
> Of rage that rises on a wing of woe,
> The old wife's wailing:
> "Whither do you go
> There is a name that you have carried far,
> My man! Have you forgotten who you are

That cowards come and drag you out of bed?
It would be well if Sitting Bull were dead
And lying in his blood! It would be well!
But now what story will be good to tell
In other winters" (85–86).

The pathetic weakness of Indian resistance to Manifest Destiny is symbolically portrayed. Sitting Bull is brutally shot, "A moment hanging slack / Amid a sag of arms, the limp form fell" (86). Sitting Bull's riderless circus horse, an ironic gift from Buffalo Bill is cued to perform by the shooting. Like a circus, military glory has been an immature expression of souls still ridden by Pride. The Ghost Dancers, far to the south in the Badlands, see a meteor signalling Sitting Bull's death. The sign is like those revealing the death of pride in both *The Scarlet Letter* and *Julius Caesar,* the last of which Neihardt might have consciously remembered in that Caesar too was a similarly benighted pagan in the eyes of the Elizabethan audience. The meteor has a clearly negative identity but its passing is a promise, Neihardt implies, of better heroes than the Hunkpapa demagogue: "Gigantic in a mist of moony flame, / He fled across the farther summits there, / That desolation of an old despair / Illumined all about him as he went. / And then, collapsing, like a runner spent, / Upon the world-rim yonder, he was gone" (88–89). The despair of this temporary light represents the convention in Christian literature of portraying characters who willfully refuse the benefits of faith and hope.

The second to last section, "The Way," is the path to Calvary and to spiritual transformation. Sitanka's Christologically phrased comfort to his freezing people promises no victories over the enemy, only salvation through transcendence of the body. The "Savior's wound grows beautiful in you," because their hearts have been "made holy with the spear" (94). The people in their suffering are privileged to leave the earth, the flesh, and time behind, to learn that good and evil cannot be chosen but that all experience, especially crucifying pain, is to be received with gratitude. Big Foot himself reveals this transformation: "For surely he grew taller by a span / And some deep well of glory over-ran / The tortured face" (95). Even as he sinks into his mortal fever, a symbol of man's passive reception of truth, "men learned to hear / . . . in the broken babble of the seer / . . . tidings of the Ever-Living Dead" (97), the promise of an eternal after-life more real than Sitting Bull's shadowland or Wovoka's earthly paradise.

Arising from his dream, Sitanka's perceptions of Christian truth are uncannily accurate for a pagan and therefore startlingly true. The spear in Christ's side prefigures the storm of bullets. The Roman soldier has become the seventh cavalry and the illumination of the Word will again be the result. Spoken just before his death, Sitanka's last sermon promises salvation for his followers. In his delirium he has become God: "A great white spear that burned into my side, / And with a voice that filled the world I cried, 'Have pity on us all, for we are blind!'" (100). The resurrection of the dead, seen by Sitanka in his dream, is even greater than Wovoka's vision, tinged as it is with revenge and separation from the whites. When the dead rise, like Hawthorne's burghers shaking off their sleep, Indian children play with soldiers "beautiful and dear." Therefore because all men are in "a blindness of the sun" (101), full of shadows, those who have seen the light and know the Word must love their enemies, "For they are brothers. Pray to understand. / Not ours alone shall be the Spirit Land. / In every heart shall bloom the Shielding Tree, / And none shall see the Savior till he see / The Stranger's face and know it for his own" (101).

Big Foot, like Christ, lives out his destined role, forgiving his enemy in the moment of death. Like the old wife distracting Sitting Bull from a progressive ascent, Yellow Bird is satanically responsible for all suffering at Wounded Knee because he forces the people to think of pride, power, and mere physical existence: "Foolish ones / And blind! Why are you giving up your guns?" (107). His words are the "final spear thrust of a cry" that passes over in the gospel paradigm of Christian poetry to become "the cry that stabbed the world with pity" (109), as Sitanka reaches out to his crucifier in whom he sees the face of

God: "He strove to rise in vain / To say 'My brother!'" (109). But the words are not actually uttered because the world is not collectively ready for salvation.

In the final blizzard that seasonally obscures the Word, the recurrence of darkness during the life of the earth is accepted. Starkloff, who condemns Neihardt as a romantic, appears to be unaware that Neihardt shares his own belief that humanity lives in constant tension between progress and primitivism. Progress in Christianity must fundamentally apply to the transformation of the fallen man of pride and aggression, the "old Adam," to the "new man," Christ, the embodiment and giver of love and salvation. Adam and Christ personify the natural and spiritual states of the human condition. "The first man is of the earth, earthy: the second man is the Lord from heaven" (I Corinthians 15:47). In his portrayal of Sitting Bull, Neihardt personifies the old Adam without benefit of Christian illumination, much as Shakespeare may have meant to explain the thought and behavior of his pre-Christian Romans in *Julius Caesar* and pre-Romanized Britons in *King Lear*.

In *The Song of the Indian Wars* (1925) which preceded *The Song of the Messiah* by ten years, Neihardt portrays the Lakota leaders as part of a dying world: "the earth was getting old and worn out" (Mooney 27). Within the Christian metaphor, the old Adam in the Indians was about to die so that they could become bearers of the power to make all new in heaven. As with Sitting Bull, the Lakota men whose names were most known to Neihardt and his readership are uniformly old, dim, and fading. Even in his greatest vitality Crazy Horse is an anachronism, a pale ghost unable to adapt to a spiritually evolving world: "A good tough horse to ride, / The gear of war, and some great dream inside / Were Crazy Horse's wealth. It seemed the dim / And larger past had wandered back in him" (*Indian Wars* 113). Crazy Horse's obvious failure implies that only Christ can shield the souls of his sheep, whose bodies are always expendable. The fundamental weakness of the non-Christian surfaces in Crazy Horse when he turns away his "brother," Dull Knife, the Cheyenne leader, who comes to him for aid when both their bands, among the last to accept confinement to a reservation, are starving in the snow. Unlike Big Foot who tries to embrace his enemy as his brother, Crazy Horse betrays the predominance of the Old Adam in his soul: "The hard lips moved: 'A man must feed his own,' / Said Crazy Horse, and turned upon his heel" (*Indian Wars* 165).

From this point of division and lovelessness, "the evil days began" and Crazy Horse "seemed no longer young" (165). The weather reflects the devolution of Lakota consciousness preceding the emergence of Christian love: "Bleak January found them on the Tongue / In search of better forage for the herd— / A failing quest" (165). In the death of Crazy Horse, Neihardt uses pathos to accentuate the tragic loss, ultimately encompassed in the divine comedy of *The Song of the Messiah*. The "vanishing" hero's death is sad but as necessary as the death of childhood in spiritual growth:

> He choked and shivered, staring hungry-eyed
> As though to make the most of little light.
> Then like a child that feels the clutching night
> And cries the wilder, deeming it in vain,
> He raised a voice made lyrical with pain
> And terror of a thing about to be.
> *"I want to see you, Father! Come to me!*
> *I want to see you, Mother!"* (178)

The "little light" is appropriate to his pre-Christian ignorance of God and heaven and explains his regressive struggle to cling to his lesser earthly life. His body is claimed by parents who, as embodiments of Lakota consciousness and religion are historically decrepit and spiritually blind. Only to those who are ghosts themselves or who mistakenly long for a dead past could Neihardt's Crazy Horse be a true hero, a potent savior. When Crazy Horse's voice is still, the true Word can be spoken: "But when at length the lyric voice was dumb / And Crazy Horse was nothing but a name, / There was a little withered woman came / Behind a bent old man. Their eyes were dim" (178).

Neihardt uses this metaphor extensively to say that the old Lakota were in the dark about their spiritual identity and purpose until they received the gospel. The Ghost Dance is both regressive in its desire for the return of the old life and progressive in its pantribal unity under a single, Christ-like messiah. When Neihardt describes the regressive aspect, that of bringing ghosts back to earth rather than meeting them in a Christian heaven, the dead souls ignorantly imagined prior to conversion, are "Dim shadow-bodies . . . / . . . swaying with a mournful sound / And feeling for remembered shadow ground / To root in—hills of fog and valleys dim" (*Messiah* 24). And when Red Cloud advises the people to continue in the Ghost Dance, he is shown to be relinquishing the old Lakota vision: "Deep voices and the women's tremolo / Acclaimed him still a mighty man and wise, / Despite the wintered hair; the rheumy eyes; / The groundward gaze, incuriously dim . . . / At length he stole away / A shadow unto shadows" (*Messiah* 45, 47).

Red Cloud returns to the darkness in which he had lived the whole span of his life, while other Lakota are given the opportunity to know the light in their physical existence. Some of the most noticeable changes made by Neihardt in the Black Elk transcript make more sense on ideological than aesthetic grounds. At the beginning of chapter 2 Neihardt's Black Elk recounts the Edenic past when the people were "seldom hungry" and lived in peace. But since the *wašicus* have forced them onto little islands (reservations), the people languish in "square gray houses" where they "starve." This turn of fortune was dreamed by a pre-contact prophet named Drinks Water who was so saddened by his vision that he soon died "and it was sorrow that killed him" (*Black Elk Speaks* 8). Neihardt significantly changes the tone of the episode. In the 1931 interview, Black Elk says that when the people live in the gray houses they will starve without their traditional religion to nourish them. Although Drinks Water does die of "regret" in the transcript, Black Elk does not conclude on an elegiac note but instead speaks of Drinks Water's ability to "make everything nearly—[he] made sugar, tobacco, matches and other things just by his words alone" (*The Sixth Grandfather* 290). At the moment of his speaking Black Elk too is using words to renew the old Lakota reality. He has not relinquished verbal power to speak for the old way as Red Cloud does in his curtain speech in *The Song of the Messiah.*

Thirteen years later in a 1944 interview with Neihardt, Black Elk's prophet has a new name and a new strength. Wooden Cup foretells the time when the people will not be in the hoop, will be entangled in iron, and will live in different tipis. Different men will make a different world with great wars, but the people will survive if they hold to the pipe and thereby receive life-giving visions (*The Sixth Grandfather* 340). Before they have seen a white man Wooden Cup appears in white man's clothes, as if to prepare the people for change and to show that a Lakota consciousness can flourish in a physically altered world. His death, unlike that of Drinks Water, instructs the people to trust in continuance and to remember that the fire in a holy man is eternally present in innumerable bodies.

Black Elk's Wooden Cup dies because he chooses to show the people how to regard death. As an advanced holy man, every act of his infuses others with balanced powers to make live, to create:

> His last wishes were that they build a big fire and burn up his body. But they did not do that; they buried him there. Where he was buried you could see a light for four days; it looked as if he were burning . . . He is about the greatest holy man of all; he is the only one I know of that had a vision about the Mysterious One. (341)

By 1944 Black Elk was fully confident of his purpose and effect. The light that burns for four days, the Lakota number of totality, burns forever. Black Elk is Wooden Cup. Others will be Black Elk as well. As the Northern spirit tells Black Elk, "hundreds shall be sacred, hundreds shall be flames" (*The Sixth Grandfather* 139).

Like Black Elk, Wooden Cup feeds the people with ceremonies in the alien context of the white man's physical trappings. Instead of fearing the white man's material culture, he appropriates it for the Lakota. He gives *wašicu* hats to twelve young men and with them they form the Owns White Society.

He ritually transforms uncontaminated dirt from a gopher hole into gunpowder as if to suggest that the spirit to maintain the people's confidence can animate a bow or a rifle, a danced expression or a computerized one (*The Sixth Grandfather* 340). In speaking to Neihardt, Black Elk, like Wooden Cup, used or "owned" the English language, as easily as the old Lakota took horses from their enemies for the people's use and survival. While Black Elk's Drinks Water is less encouragingly active than his Wooden Cup of thirteen years later, Neihardt's corresponding character bearing that name has no power other than to experience defeat and, in the Christian sense of suicide, "die of grief." With consistency if not recognition, Starkloff identifies Neihardt's personal attitudes toward the historical tragedy as being like Drinks Water's and quite different from his own. The new Christian Lakota Church "cannot be one of weeping old men with only memories to live on, beautiful as these are" (Starkloff 171). Perhaps if Starkloff had read *The Song of the Messiah,* he would have recognized in it his own religious concept of grief as the antithesis of Christian hope.

Neihardt believed that the despair of the Old Adam throughout the world would gradually be assuaged as God granted each nation truth and salvation according to his wisdom and in his own time. When Starkloff recommends that *Black Elk Speaks* be read to "show how 'the seeds of the Word' grow slowly and gradually within a unique culture like the Lakota" (160), he is not only expressing the main theme of *The Song of the Messiah,* but also Neihardt's purpose in revising Black Elk's words. Using the primary metaphor of the Word, both men work for a common purpose.

But if Starkloff and Neihardt are in implicit agreement as to Neihardt's theology, DeMallie thinks *Black Elk Speaks* is an "elegy" composed by Neihardt to commemorate the passing of a great people. Actually, *Black Elk Speaks* was not written in a state of mind radically different from the one that wrote *The Song of the Messiah* only four years later. While DeMallie considers Neihardt as a humanist and a mystic, a closer examination of the texts of both of his major works discloses a relatively doctrinaire Christian message. DeMallie so ignores this theme as to state that the slaughter at Wounded Knee was caused "by the unbending opposition of the whites" ("Lakota Legacy" 125), This is like saying that bad people crucified Christ, as opposed to recognizing the event as an apopemptic fulfillment of a providential plan, at least in Neihardt's theological context. Similarly, DeMallie thinks Sitanka realizes only the oneness of humankind, even though Neihardt could not be more explicit about locating this unity in Christ.

Even more seriously misleading, however, is DeMallie's omission of Neihardt's Christianity when he compares *Black Elk Speaks* to the original transcript in his extensive introduction to *The Sixth Grandfather*. Without clarification of Neihardt's representatively Christian beliefs, the Lakota religion cannot be explained very well in the English language to a readership generally ignorant of both that religion and the premises of Western belief. DeMallie thinks that the differences between these religions are "petty," and that Neihardt grew experientially in *The Song of the Messiah,* until the Lakota and Western perspectives became "inextricably intertwined in him" ("Lakota Legacy" 133). If anything, however, Neihardt's last work is his most Christian and least Lakota, the Lakota integrity of *Black Elk Speaks* existing only to the extent that Neihardt felt he could not betray Black Elk (*The Sixth Grandfather* 29, 51). But in *The Song of the Messiah* Neihardt is unrestrained and expresses a vision entirely Western in conception and metaphor.

DeMallie, respected for his knowledge of Lakota tradition, attempts to discover the effects of Black Elk's own Christianity upon the Neihardt interviews. In regard to Black Elk's being led to see the sacred hoop embracing all peoples during his Great Vision, DeMallie adds with caution: "he seems to have interpreted it as a promise of salvation for all peoples within the harmony of the sacred circle" (*The Sixth Grandfather* 89). He goes on correctly to state, "Salvation, of course, is a Christian concept" (89–90). But then DeMallie goes out on a limb:

Traditional Lakotas felt no such need, for they considered themselves the original and best people. The emphasis on salvation may arise in part out of Black Elk's fear that the

Indian people would pass away completely, overpowered by the whites. In part it may reflect his later interpretations in light of the Christian doctrine of salvation. (90)

Just as Neihardt occasionally puts words in Black Elk's mouth, DeMallie contradicts evidence presented by the very transcript he has edited. Black Elk does not interpret the sacred hoop as international unity. He looks into the cup of the western grandfather and sees "different tribes that I was to get along with on earth" (*The Sixth Grandfather* 138). Later he looks into the cup of the sixth grandfather, the spirit of the earth, who instructs him to help the struggling people he sees by "making six centers of the nation's hoop" for the Hunkpapa, Minneconjou, Sicangu (Brulé), Oglalas, Cheyenne, and No Bows, all of whom compose the nation he is to renew: "Behold them, this is your nation and you shall go back to them" (*The Sixth Grandfather* 140–41). Nowhere does Black Elk speak of different peoples as unified but only as people with whom he will make some sort of alliance on behalf of his own people.

This is far from the unity in Christ of barbarian, Scythian, or Jew (Colossians 3:11). DeMallie is subjectively frank to use the word "seems" in attributing a salvational tone to these passages since Black Elk clearly speaks to unite his own people and to get along with others. To say that traditional Lakota felt no need for salvation may be true, but not because they considered themselves the "best people." Traditional Lakota would not have believed any people to require salvation because they did not believe in Original Sin (see Ramsey 171). From saying that Black Elk "seems" to be propounding salvation, DeMallie jumps to Black Elk's "emphasis on salvation" (*The Sixth Grandfather* 90), arising from his supposed "fear that the Indian people would pass away completely, overpowered by the whites" (90).

Neither Black Elk's universalism nor a belief in salvation (essential tenets of Christianity) exist in the text of Neihardt's transcript in the prominence inferred by DeMallie. Black Elk's Catholicism is essentially a historical fact, exterior to his communication to Neihardt, though far more in evidence in his religiously syncretic description of Lakota ceremonies in *The Sa-*

cred Pipe. In that work Black Elk consciously adjusts Lakota religious concepts and metaphors to make them sympathetic and comprehensible to a Christian audience. But in his interviews with Neihardt in 1931 and 1944, Lakota culture is presented for itself without the Christian shading DeMallie, usually so meticulous in his analyses, inexplicably projects upon the text.

In *The Sixth Grandfather* Black Elk does not think eschatologically. His story says that human life must be lived within the hoop and on the earth. When Drinks Water or Wooden Cup say the Lakota will not live in the hoop, they mean both the physical circle of tipis and the Lakota seasonal pattern of natural possibility. In Black Elk's vision the tree flowers on the earth, because the spirits direct their efforts there. The Christian good news is that the tree on which Christ, the fruit of life hangs, permits human beings to leave the hoop forever for a better home. Neihardt was sympathetic to Black Elk's dream to retain the related tribes in a Lakota hoop, but he considered it regressive. While he includes references to some Lakotas' contemplated cannibalism after the Custer fight, as something the Indians were in their primitive past (*Black Elk Speaks* 127), he changes Black Elk's description of Lakota unity to a prophecy of universal peace as if to indicate a moral progression brought about by God: "And I saw that the sacred hoop of my people was one of many hoops that made one circle, wide as daylight and as starlight, and in the center grew one mighty flowering tree to shelter all the children of one mother and one father. And I saw that it was holy" (*Black Elk Speaks* 43). As Neihardt's revision begins in Eden, it ends on Calvary. None of the imagery is Black Elk's, from the parentage of Adam and Eve to the redemptive drops of blood on the white body of the snow, an image of anticipation mixed with sorrow in the context of the promised end. Although "a people's dream died there," a greater awakening will follow.

In the tradition of European depiction of pagan limitations, Black Elk was not privileged to know that the nation's hoop must providentially break, and the first Edenic tree die so that it could become the tree of life beyond the earth. In the Postscript a benevolent God no longer allows the Lakota religion to serve its old purpose. Black Elk can bring only (in Neihardt's phrasing) "a scant, chill rain" with his Lakota prayer. Christian prayers have made his obsolete. He leaves "silent" and "weeping in the drizzling rain" (*Black Elk Speaks* 274). Forty years later Neihardt could observe that Black Elk might not have failed to restore the hoop after all "with his message spreading across the world" (1972 Pocket Books edition xiii), but in 1931 his thinking was polished into a centuries-old typology. Starkloff's "weeping old men" are regarded somewhat more coldly than Neihardt's, but the same self-conscious condescension toward them appears in an excess of pitying adjectives: "We who listened now noted that thin clouds had gathered about us. A scant chill rain began to fall and there was low, muttering thunder without lightning. With tears running down his cheeks, the old man raised his voice to a thin high wail, and chanted" (*Black Elk Speaks* 274). Sad as this may be, all tragedy in traditional Christian literature must be regarded as transitional.

FIVE

Shaped by Ritual:
The Enactment of
Black Elk's Visions

WHILE Christianity recommends prayer to absolve sin and guarantee bliss beyond the grave, Lakota religion enhances life on earth through ritual disciplines. Power is usually a knowledge of symbols and their proper use. Since the primary spiritual concern is always creation rather than salvation, it is not surprising that early missionaries like the Congregationalist Samuel Pond wrote in 1838 of the Dakota in Minnesota, "I can tell them many things concerning the character and government of God, but [I] cannot preach Christ crucified" (S. Pond xv). Like the twentieth century Jesuits, Stolzman and Starkloff, and like Neihardt, Pond believed that the Dakota religion was "rather vague and defective than erroneous . . . its convictions . . . the remains of a clearer light which they had once possessed . . . the natural suggestions of reason and conscience" (S. Pond 108).

Their conscience made "wrong" a matter of interfering with supernatural action by neglecting or improperly performing rituals. Pond implicitly regards this as immature compulsiveness: "the smoking of the wrong pipe, or at the wrong time, might provoke them more than theft or murder" (108). The Lakota did not ignore intratribal crimes, though they did not make their punishment the central symbol of security, as in Western culture. Murder was dealt with practically, through banishment, or ritually, through vengeance carried out by the victim's relatives (see E. Deloria, *Speaking of Indians* 23). The courtroom drama did not exist to give the larger society of beholders a satisfying image of themselves. Rather, the breaking of ritual order offended because it slackened willingness to sustain the health of the group. Rituals kept the people focused on the qualities of mind and body that made survival possible.

After the Great Vision has established the values and fulfillment of a Lakota existence, Black Elk repeatedly recalls how a thoroughly ritualized life made the Great Vision's promise immediately known. Food is not thoughtlessly taken and consumed but remembered as a gift of the grandfathers. Although only a few scouts ride out to search for buffalo, their killing, butchering, and consuming is a ritual performed by the whole tribe. The voice of a single crier consistently represents a unity of purpose and effort: "There were scouts sent out ahead of them to find buffalo. The crier says: 'Many buffalo I have heard, many buffalo I have heard. Your children, you must take care of them' (Meaning to keep the children close to them while traveling so they wouldn't scare the buffalo)" (*The Sixth Grandfather* 144). Then when the scouts return, the crier again represents all those individual acts that together express the people's power to live: "The crier came out and said: 'Come forth and make haste. I have protected you; in return you shall give many things' (speaking for the scouts)" (*The Sixth Grandfather* 145).

The scouts' report is performed as sacred drama in which the chiefs and scouts follow a prescribed outline, varying only in the specific physical circumstances of the information which is not simply given but ritually repeated:

> Then the chief said the same thing again: "I will be thankful to you. Tell me fully what you have seen out there. It shall be the truth." And the scout said: "On the other side of that last herd there is nothing but buffalo all over the country." The chief said: "*Hetchetu alo*" (It is so indeed) (*The Sixth Grandfather* 146).

This drama is then transferred intact to the voice of the crier who in turns transmits it to the people. The crier extends the sacredness of the process to the next phase, preparing for the hunt. His words are not necessary in a practical sense, since the people know what to do after the buffalo have been located. The recitation serves to make them appreciative of an existence their culture prevents them from blunting: "Your knives must be sharpened, your arrows shall be sharpened. Make ready, make haste, your horses make ready. We shall go forth with your arrows. Plenty of meat we shall make" (*The Sixth Grandfather* 146).

The ritualizing of physical necessity helps to create an existence of joy and meaning. When the Lakota killed animals, they usually left part of the individual carcass (often the head, feet and tail) as an offering to the generalized spirit of that species to show appreciation and to establish kinship, so that the particular species would agree to die for them. While Black Elk and his father are hunting, Black Elk implicitly compares hunting rituals to all creative activity when he tells his father that patience is more important than pursuit:

> "No, father, you stay here, they are bringing them toward us and we'll get them here." When I realized what I had said, it made me feel queer for I thought this was also a part of my vision . . . So father lay down in some high grass and watched . . . I went back and held the horses . . . and I heard two shots and knew that my father had gotten two antelopes . . . After . . . my father [went] down to the antelopes, he found out that he had shot four antelopes with two shots. (*The Sixth Grandfather* 155)

After the kill, Black Elk again ensures the coming of more game by feeling pity rather than triumph. Such an habitual response is also conducive to harmonious relationships in the camp circle and in vision-seeking. Spirits and people will empathize rather than struggle with each other. Existence is lived to distribute and circulate health and awareness. Black Elk's father leaves one of the two antelopes: "To all the wild things that eat flesh, / This I have offered that my people may live and the children will grow up in abundance" (*The Sixth Grandfather* 156).

Rituals feed the people with a loving appreciation of what existence brings and with the strength to survive difficulty. Rather than delivering its believers from fear, Lakota religion accepts the necessity of fear as a phase in the evolution of the power to renew. The Great Vision is followed by the historical journey of the Lakota through the four ascents. After the death of Crazy Horse and the return from Canada, Lakota physical strength and morale were severely weakened. Black Elk's visionary identity returns to him, as it always returns when survival seems most threatened. However, the extreme fear Black Elk feels is not of the whites but the Thunder beings who require him to bring their potentially explosive energy into himself and through him into the camp circle. By enacting his vision in the horse dance, the people are freed from fear because they become Thunder beings themselves. The horse nation that "arrives" at the dance is the Thunder spirit emerging in the people.

The transformation is brought about through a convergence of various sensory expressions that actualize the qualities of the symbols in participants and beholders, making them symbols as well. The major symbols of Black Elk's vision are painted on the sacred tipi by two old men, Bear Sings and Black Road, as if to show how their powers are transmitted through human beings. The tipi itself is a symbol of the forms that contain human consciousness, and over the entrance the rainbow is the totality of expression the spirits have generally granted to be continually returned to the people. The rainbow does not banish fear but rather exists as a more developed phase of the elements of fear. Fear is inseparable from the energy of expression. Before the dance begins, the horses were painted so that they "looked beautiful, but still they looked fearful" (*The Sixth Grandfather* 217).

The ritual introduction of fear is a necessary infusion of the force that will become the power to grow (see chapter 6). An actual thunder storm contributes to this meaning, sending the people to fasten down their tipis, but finally dropping only a little sprinkle on the dance itself. The black horse riders incarnate the emergence of courage from fear. Facing the storm, they let it sensorily suffuse them until they can sing of thunder in the first person: "I myself, made them fear. / Myself I wore an eagle relic. / . . . Myself a lightning power I wore. / . . . Myself, hail-like powers I wore. / . . . I, myself, made them fear. / Behold me!" (220).

Lakota symbolic thought responds to the source of fear by empathizing with it. Sometimes the source is a single danger-ous animal like the bear (see chapter 6) or the buffalo, but the most frightening Lakota beings are the Thunders, especially their single personification as Wakinyan, the Thunder bird (see Walker, *Lakota Myth* 213). Anyone who sees the Thunder bird in a dream or vision will be beset by such extreme fears that he must become a *heyoka* clown, one who humiliates himself to show how losses can be endured. Black Elk becomes a *heyoka* as a result of his Dog vision, which comes to him on a formal *hanbleceya* or vision quest. The extremity of a *heyoka's* sacrifice of normal caution and pride is in direct proportion to the danger of inflating these qualities.

Black Elk's Dog vision comes at a time when Lakota pride has been subdued. Even the most resistant bands are on reserva-tions, the last to surrender being Sitting Bull's Hunkpapas with whom Black Elk lived in Canada before starvation and cold forced them to assume residence at Fort Yates, North Dakota. Black Elk returned to his own people at Pine Ridge to find them in despair in comparison to the Hunkpapas who had been cheered by the horse dance. In the spring the Thunder beings make themselves heard and to Black Elk they are saying, "It is time to perform the duties of your grandfathers," i.e., perform the horse dance (*The Sixth Grandfather* 229). The vision that en-ables Black Elk to continue what that ceremony began does not happen spontaneously like the Great Vision.

Hanbleceya is a formal, ritual pattern requiring preparation, discipline, and intense concentration from the "lamenters" or vision-seekers (see *The Sacred Pipe* 44–56). The one who under-takes this rite does the work of the grandfathers in that he receives power from the spirits to help generate new life. The formal seeking must be continually repeated, especially by medicine men, and although Black Elk's Great Vision has already effected transformation in the horse dance, more symbolic expression must be added to his curative practice:

> In this year when the tender faces of the grass appeared I could hear the Thunder beings coming again under the earth. I had not yet completed the duties assigned me by my vision to be a medicine man. I could hear the Thunder beings say: "It is time to fulfill what your grandfathers have assigned you." (*The Sixth Grandfather* 227)

Black Elk's "longing" for spring may intuitively express the collective feeling of reservation existence before the revival of Lakota religion, as well as any period in which human beings are deprived of wisdom symbolically expressed. The preparatory sweat lodge manifests immediate receptiveness in the individual. The seeker must be emptied of pride or despair so that he can be "pitied"; spirits give their wisdom only to those who know they cannot live without it. The heat releases resistance so that the lamenter can surrender to beings more powerful than he. All he can do is pray and wait.

Then the formal patterning and repetition of prayers in sequence to the directions further focuses the mind, while the formal "crying," for which the rite is named, induces the individual powerlessness that makes spiritual infusion possible. Black Elk's tears become real when he thinks of his dead relatives, though he never says that he wishes he were dead himself. Neihardt put these words in his mouth: "I thought it might be better if my crying would kill me; then I could be in the outer world where nothing is ever in despair" (*Black Elk Speaks* 154). In the transcript Black Elk is neither suicidal nor Platonic, saying only that he cried a great deal: "I recalled the days when all my close relatives had been living and now they were gone. I just cried myself to death nearly" (*The Sixth Grandfather* 228). References to the outer world also reflect Neihardt's interest in the Ghost Dance, but the Dog vision reflects the traditional use of ritual to benefit the dreamer's people in this world:

I saw . . . beautiful butterflies of all kinds hovering over me . . . and the spotted eagle spoke to me saying: "Behold them, these are your people." These little butterflies of all colors seemed to be crying . . . The spotted eagle spoke again, saying: "These people shall be in great difficulty and you shall go there." (*The Sixth Grandfather* 228–29)

The butterflies, as *akicita* (messengers) of the western powers (see *The Sixth Grandfather* 99), repeat the transformation of the people from beholders of the thunder at the horse dance to embodiments of the thunder:

Then just as they disappeared, the chicken hawk said to me: "Behold your grandfathers shall come forth and you shall hear them." I lifted up my head and there was a great storm coming. The Thunder being nation was coming and I could hear the voices over there and the neighing of horses and the sending of voices and I knew they were coming in a sacred manner. It was a fearful sight but I just stood there. (*The Sixth Grandfather* 229)

Far from continuing to cry, the butterflies, joined by dragonflies, swarm around a dog just before the two men who initiated the Great Vision swoop down from the clouds to spear the dog's head "up in the air" with their arrows.

Neihardt makes the message simplistically political by doubling the dogs and having their heads turn into *wašicus'* heads after they are speared (*Black Elk Speaks* 185), but Black Elk himself meant the killing to express the transformation of abject helplessness into ritual remediation:

The dog's head transformed into a man's head. The heart of the dog turned into the heart of a man. You will remember that in the first vision I had they wanted me to kill a dog, and in this I now knew what I was to do by getting the understanding of that power to be performed on this earth . . . The dog is timid and . . . is used as the material for the performance of lots of ceremonials . . . When a dog is used for ceremonial purposes, it is called sacred eating and it will make clarity of understanding. (*The Sixth Grandfather* 229–30)

The expression of fear during *hanbleceya* maintains the momentum of man's return to his strongest, fullest self. Only after Black Elk truly fears for his life in the midst of the storm does calm strength envelop him. That inner strength is externalized by the phenomenon of spiritual invulnerability, which is also contributed to the story in the horse dance by the same powers that prevent hail and rain from falling in the sacred space of the *hanbleceya* circle. Again the answer to fear is expressed in a rainbow image, this time an herb radiating light of many colors near the people "all sad and weary . . . A voice said: 'Your people are in difficulty. Make haste. They need you.' Just then this voice woke me up as I was noticing the herb" (*The Sixth Grandfather* 230–31). Then in the transcript, but not in *Black Elk Speaks,* Black Elk refers to the dominant purpose of Lakota religion. Vision at first extends experience beyond safe boundaries, but soon the seeker learns that his power will protect him wherever he and the people must travel: "I had seen so much that night that I should have been scared, but I was not in fear" (*The Sixth Grandfather* 231). Returning to a world, in which no human being is sustained at every moment by immediate spiritual aid, necessitates a concluding sweat lodge ceremony, wherein older men, who have themselves repeated this journey, instruct Black Elk to share his power with the people in the *heyoka* ceremony.

His vision of the Thunder beings requires Black Elk to become a *heyoka* or sacred clown, who reveals the truth by enacting it consistently in reverse: "When the vision comes from the west, it comes in terror like a thunder storm, but when the storm of [the] vision has passed, the whole world is green and happy as a result. In the ceremony of the *heyoka* this order is reversed, the creation of the happy frame of mind in the people preceding the presentation of the truth" (232). The clowns' transformation is initially represented by the painless killing of a dog, performed as a ritual and followed by the further rituals of butchering, washing, and boiling.

As the dog in the pot changes from a slave animal to a being that feeds and enlightens the people, the *heyoka* do their foolish tricks to recommend trust in the spirits: "the whole right side of the hair [was] shaved off their heads, the left side hanging loose and long . . . the hair was cut on the right side . . . for humility to the west" (233). Because they respect the most fearful powers of all, they can mock ordinary fears. First they pretend to measure the depth of a mud puddle by placing arrows horizontally on it. Thus the completely soaked arrow proves the puddle to be far over their heads, immediately provoking a typical *heyoka* act when one of them suddenly "plunges" in and pretends to drown only to be rescued by another (234). This excessive expenditure of energy is immediately answered by the central symbol of growth from dog to man, clown to healer. The heart and head of the dog are speared in the pot by Black Elk and One Side as they gallop past on horseback, salvaging the essential spiritual qualities, the basic purpose of most ceremonies. With the wasteful thoughts and actions (previously enacted by the *heyoka*) purified away, the people can all share in the dog flesh made sacred in the ceremony. If a dog can be made sacred in the symbolic imagination, so can any ordinary human being.

Neihardt omits the arrival of a thunder storm near the end of the ceremony, perhaps to avoid redundancy or confusion with the storm that occurs during the horse dance. But the *heyoka* and horse dance storms are not identical. While the people share in the spiritualized dog meat, circulating the Thunder power within them, "the Thunder beings were coming again in a thunder storm with full force and the hail was coming from the west and before it came to the gathering it spread and went on both sides, but once in a while you could see a few hail pieces falling near" (235). Although Black Elk does not explain, this storm demonstrates the efficacy of the ceremony and is its culmination.

The horse dance and the *heyoka* ceremony attract the thunder, the major source of fear. The Lakota religion therefore involves risk. To have the strength to survive, one must fully accept one's weakness. But the weakness is never conceived as moral weakness. The spirits, unlike Christ, do not pity man because he is unable to keep the moral law. Man's weakness does not come from sin but from his inability to transcend individual concern and its resultant vulnerability. The most frequently sung Lakota prayer is the pipe song which promises a larger identification with the creative source of being as well as the power to manifest what that source imparts: "Kola lecel econ wo/ . . . Heconun kin/ Nitunkaśila waniyang u kte lo" 'Friend, do it like this/ . . . If you do [load the pipe properly and pray] / Your grandfather will come to see you" (Around Him and White Hat, Sr. 10).

Black Elk is brought to the creative power, as in the song, so that he can learn to speak and in speech fulfill the people's needs. The first and last verses of the song quoted above are identical and complete the circle of human purpose. Man at his best is a grandfather recreating the consciousness of the people in sensory forms he risks his lesser identity to obtain. Trouble is inevitable and healing comes through symbols, which in turn generate a further creation of symbols in the one who receives them. The Great Vision comes unsought as if to affirm an alliance to the spirits, but Black Elk like any ordinary human being must rigorously seek subsequent visions. The spirits act beyond human understanding, sometimes sending wisdom to the most unlikely recipients. But Black Elk's Great Vision is consistent with the spirits' responding immediately to the weak and humble for their greater receptiveness, and any lamenter must be in some sense a sick child, as Black Elk was.

SIX

Black Elk and Lakota Healing

L AKOTA healing ceremonies almost invariably include an ordeal, simultaneously real and symbolic, emphatically felt by all present. Invisible powers that have entered the doctor in a vision are evoked by the ceremony to transfer strength to the patient. Health is usually associated with wisdom, the confidence that allows the body and the spirit to return to equilibrium without inhibition or panic. To free the recipient of a curing ceremony from fear, the "story" must produce fear. It must make the patient or reader identify with the whole story, not just the happy ending. For the person or group who suffers, the treatment begins in ritualized aggravation that demonstrates the ability to endure. Before Black Elk's Great Vision begins, he is a sick child and he feels fear as the messenger of the Thunder takes him to the sky. He becomes desperate eight years later when the Thunder beings plague him until he learns that he must enact his vision through the horse dance. And finally the fear he feels during his *heyoka* vision is intense, helping him to remember the spirits who alone maintain the powers he has previously been given.

An early lesson in the value of ritualized fear comes from Hairy Chin, the Bear medicine healer whom Black Elk assists when he is still young and impressionable (*The Sixth Grandfather* 178–79). The bear healers were adept at curing broken bones as well as various maladies (Hassrick 291). Bushotter tells us of their selection and high regard: "Those men who dream the bear spirit, are thereby consecrated; and whatever they undertake they achieve without fail" (E. Deloria, *Teton Myths*

199). The qualities of these givers of life, however, are paradoxical. At the meetings of the Bear dreamers, "those who are to dance suddenly grow sharp teeth; and when this happens they are not themselves, and no matter what they lay hold on they bite it to pieces or scratch it all up, by clawing it" (E. Deloria, *Teton Myths* 199). Closely associated with the fearfulness and fearlessness evoked by the bear men is the miraculous ability to dissolve the threat they have intentionally brought to the sick (see Wissler, 88–91). They find a medicine invisible to those without their vision: "when these men dance, they draw forth a wild turnip out of the ground . . . and then they pass it about among those who are ailing, so each one takes a piece, and are healed thereby. Some of the bear-actors sit with blood streaming out of their mouths" (E. Deloria, *Teton Myths* 199).

Black Elk too uses an herb known only to him from his vision, and while he never appears with blood on his face, his herb is associated with the Thunder beings who miraculously appear at the horse dance, an event in which beneficial fear verges into joy for the kinship confirmed with these tremendous spirits. DeMallie has thoroughly shown the ways in which Black Elk's vision comes from the western powers, an emphasis obscured by Neihardt (*The Sixth Grandfather* 3–7, 54, 86, 99). The latter also omitted Black Elk's reception of a blue man into his body, another spirit bestowed by the grandfathers to assist in healing. Black Elk uses the blue man when engaged in sucking out a patient's sickness (*The Sixth Grandfather* 121, 139). This practice implicitly teaches the patient that he cannot resist the anger or the assistance of the spirits. Even the healer has no special strength of his own. Without the blue man Black Elk would be like Bushotter's bear healer who "faints" when "the bear spirit comes out of . . . his mouth in the form of a bear cub" and does not awaken until the bear cub returns. And this conception of curative cause was applied to many varieties of animal dreamers: "It was said that those various birds or animals which resided within the doctor's body were really the power behind him . . . he would turn to the holy being inside him for aid, and that would reply by giving a cry or call; and then the doctoring became efficacious, they say" (E. Deloria, *Teton Myths* 109).

This complete dependence on spirit helpers has been expressed by Frank Fools Crow, the most well known and highly respected of Black Elk's successors. Fools Crow's first vision was as extraordinary for a young man as that of Black Elk. In it he was given all of the 405 good spirits in the universe, the "Stone White Man helpers . . . who perform the great things through my mind and body" (Mails, *Fools Crow* 50). One group of these spirits teaches the use of herbs and plants for physical health; another shows how herbs can be used to sharpen perceptions; a third uses medicines to promote dreams that will help the dreamer to cure himself; and the last helps the medicine man to know and convey spiritual mysteries (Mails, *Fools Crow* 50).

Curing transfers an essence of the medicine man's power to the patient, to his audience. Thomas Tyon, the mixed blood interpreter upon whom Walker extensively relied, told him: "Many men are wounded by bullets or the like; the Bear doctors make all of them well. So those who have been wounded and made well by the Bear doctors are taken into the Bear group" (*Lakota Belief and Ritual* 157; see also Buechel, "Diary" 5–27–15). In this particular account the Lakota cycle of knowing one's weakness before coming into effective strength is enacted by healers with an extraordinary potential to destroy. By introducing fear into the patient and witnesses, the doctors are able to redirect its energy. The danger is isolated, exposed, and its momentum circles to preserve the person instead of blocking the impulse of the body and the mind toward natural restoration. At first the "story" is soothing, full of comfort and promise. The bear doctors offer an aromatic white medicine to the wounded to inhale and when they do, "the wounds do not fester" (*Lakota Belief and Ritual* 158). But the ceremony is not completed with physical restoration. It must also renew trust in the spirits among all members of the community: "Suddenly the Bear leader begins to move quickly towards the tipi entrance. Growling ferociously, he comes out of the tipi. His body is painted entirely red and his hands white; he carries a knife. All of the onlookers flee" (*Lakota Belief and Ritual* 158; see also Sword's description of bear healing in DeMallie, "Lakota Belief and Ritual" 40–41).

When a recovered man follows the leader to demonstrate his reception of some of his superhuman vitality, he carries a red stick, just as Rattling Hawk does in Black Elk's bear healing (*The Sixth Grandfather* 179). The stick embodies the invisible support that permits him to walk, to believe in his own strength. More power is manifested as the bear singers emerge behind him, "singing as loudly as they can." As if the singers represent the unity of the leader and the wounded men who preceded him, now the two formerly separate beings, one strong and one weak, act as one strong being: "Therefore, the Bear leader and the one who was wounded bend down and move about furiously" (Walker, *Lakota Belief and Ritual* 158). Both are inhabited by the bear spirit and all who depend on this power need have no fear for themselves as individuals since they know they are capable of protecting each other from enemies or sickness: "Perhaps the spectators standing there have a dog. If the knife bearer sees it, he chases it and if it is unwell, he overtakes it and immediately tears it to pieces and even though it is raw, he, the Bear leader, that is, eats it" (Walker, *Lakota Belief and Ritual* 158). This ingestion, like that of the healer who swallows a spirit, is empathically shared. Receiving wholeness through the eyes rather than the mouth, "the wounded begin to walk and they stand facing the south. Then they turn and stand facing the west. Again they turn and stand facing the north. Again they turn and they stand facing the east. They all stand with their arms raised in prayer. Throughout they sing the songs" (Walker, *Lakota Belief and Ritual* 158). The songs make explicit the narrative aspect of healing in this particular ceremony.

The voice sends the healing power into the sick through the ears. A healing root is then applied directly to the wounds. Tyon adds that the sense of being protected by mysterious powers is augmented through the motion of the body, the spatial relation to the healers, even the feeling of the wind as they walk: "When the Bear society is moving (*iklakapi*), the wounded ones walk ahead of the others. When they move, they walk and nobody goes before them. The wounded never go against the wind. They carefully see to this" (Walker, *Lakota Belief and Ritual* 159). The future bear must learn to overcome fear by trusting completely in spirit helpers. He must first be wounded to know his vulnerability, and he must then be cured by realizing the religious mystery necessary for survival. The story, enacted in the ritual, shows the beholders that personal suffering creates human beings capable of protecting and transforming the people: "So not just anyone takes part in the Bear society. It is because a Bear doctor has caused him to live that a man takes part in the society. There are many doctors but this is the way the Bear doctors increase in number. Therefore, the bear doctor songs are very good" (Walker, *Lakota Belief and Ritual* 159).

Walker's associate, George Sword, also emphasizes the idea of songs as medicine. But "if the wrong song or invocation is used, the medicine will do no good" (*Lakota Belief and Ritual* 91). Sound is as important to healing as other sensory media, ingested, inhaled, or applied to the skin. Sword mentions a drum and rattle first in a description of a medicine man's tools. Both a *pejuta wicaśa* (medicine man) and a *wicaśa wakan* (holy man) use songs but while the medicine man uses herbal medicine with his songs, the holy man depends on his ceremonial bag which "has a mystery in it and this mystery makes the bag very potent. It has all the potency of the mystery . . . Or it may be anything that is revealed to him in a vision" (*Lakota Belief and Ritual* 92; see also Powers, *Sacred Language* 179, 195).

The holy man's *wakan* helper is concentrated in a *sicun,* an object radiating invisible medicine. Both bag and object are symbolic containers, representing the necessity of physical embodiment in implementing spiritual action. And as the bag can be seen and touched, the song that releases its invisible power must be sensorily known. These non-dualistic, non-Christian uses of the physical world activate the spiritual momentum that will make the patient whole. The bag is not full, the song is short, leaving room for the spirits to act within the circle of consciousness cleansed by the rite. Unlike shamans of other tribes, Lakota healers do not use symbols to command spirits (see Sandner 105–6, 259–60), but rather they "prepare a place" (Fools Crow,

South Dakota Oral History Tape 453). If the ceremonial setting is meticulously completed, showing complete trust in the efficacy of the spirits, they may choose to enter the circle. Their arrival is often precipitated by a song: "Then when he sings this song and says these words, the bag will do as he bids. It is not the bag which does this but that which is in the bag. This is called *sicun* in Lakota. The bag is called *wasicun*" (Walker *Lakota Belief and Ritual* 92).

The concept of *sicun* is essential to understanding much Lakota symbolism. *Sicun* is power embodied in a material form, such as a *wotawe,* an arrangement of feathers and other objects attached to the body when going to war (Walker, *Lakota Belief and Ritual* 264–65; see also Blish 295; E. Deloria, *Teton Myths* 210–11). While the Lakota did not call a story or a curative song a *sicun,* the sense of objectifying immeasurable power in a compressed, accessible form corresponds in varied cultural expressions. Sword adds that many holy men were also medicine men and used herbal remedies in certain instances. Both Black Elk and Fools Crow employ every available medium of concentrating and directing curative effect.

Nevertheless, some healers preferred specialization, as Shooter told Densmore:

> In the old days the Indians had few diseases, and so there was not a demand for a large variety of medicines. A medicine man usually treated one special disease and treated it successfully. He did this in accordance with his dream. A medicine man would not try to dream of *all* herbs and treat *all* diseases, for then he could not expect to succeed in all nor to fulfill properly the dream of any one herb or animal. He would depend on too many and fail in all. That is one reason why our medicine men lost their power when so many diseases came among us with the advent of the white man. (245)

A clear definition was given by these early informants of the *wakanhan,* holy men who healed with *sicun,* commanded stones to find lost objects or people, brought good weather, or directed the sun dance, and other ceremonies. These men were distinguished from the *wapiye* who "conjured the sick," and the *pejuta wicaśa* (root or herb men) who cured with physical medicines. As Walker had learned from Sword, Densmore was informed that a man might use more than one of these methods (as Black Elk did), "but he was best known by the one which he employed the most" (245; see also E. Deloria, *Teton Myths* 413).

The sucking cure, a power given to Black Elk in the Great Vision (*The Sixth Grandfather* 239), is described in more detail in Densmore than in Bushotter (see also Buechel, "Diary" 4–17–15). The descent into fear is immediately accomplished by the doctor before the long ascent to well-being can begin:

> Then he came toward me, still beating his drum. As he came near me his breath was so forcible it seemed as if it would blow me before it. Just before he reached me, and while blowing his breath so strongly, he struck his body on the right side and the left side. He was still telling his dream and singing, but when he paused for an instant I could hear the sound of a red hawk; some who were there even said they could see the head of a red hawk coming out of his mouth. He bent over me and I expected that he would suck the poison from my body with his mouth, but instead I felt the beak of a bird over the place where the pain was. It penetrated so far that I could feel the feathers of the bird. The medicine man kept perfectly still for a time; then he got up with a jerk to signify that he had gotten out the trouble. Still it was the beak of a bird which I felt. A boy stood near, holding a filled pipe. It was soon apparent that the medicine man had swallowed the poison. He took four whiffs of the pipe. Then he must get rid of the poison. This part of the performance was marked by great activity and pounding of the drum. At times he kicked the bare ground in his effort to get rid of the poison; he paced back and forth, stamped his feet, and used both rattle and drum. Finally he ejected the poison into the wooden bowl. Then he told the people that he had sucked out all the poison, that none remained in my body, and that I would recover.
>
> Opening his medicine bag, he took out some herbs and placed them in a cup of cold water. He stirred it up and told

me to drink it and to repeat the dose next morning, and that in less than ten days I would be well. I did as he told me, and in about 10 days I was entirely well. (247–48)

The doctor has received the hawk into himself and his ceremony allows the hawk to withdraw the sickness. The man's song becomes that of the hawk, as health comes with perception. To be sick is to be oblivious to mysterious beings, while health accompanies the sick one's coming to an immediate knowledge of supernatural presence. Before the actions that precipitate the hawk's emergence, the medicine man begins to alter negative reality by "telling a story," by using words and drum beats to create a reality which will be completed in the dramatic acts of his ceremony:

> Beating the drum rapidly with the rattle, he said: "Young man, try to remember what I tell you. You shall see the power from which I have the right to cure sicknesses, and this power shall be used on you this day." Then he told the dream by which he received his power as a medicine man. When he rose to his feet I noticed that a horse's tail hung at his side, being fastened to his belt. Standing, he offered his drum to the cardinal points, then beat it as hard as he could, sometimes louder, sometimes softer. A wooden bowl which he carried was placed next my head. (Densmore 247).

As the hawk's beak penetrates the stomach to the source of weakness, music enters the ears to vitalize the body. To heal in such an unaccustomed way was dangerous. The Lakota understood that symbolic power can be threatened by skepticism, by a narrow practicality that obscures the other world. Accordingly, Iktomi, the trickster spirit of sterile competition and hedonism, must be kept away from ceremonial objects. The mind he personifies is contagious and can neutralize power because it does not value the benefit to persistence and awareness that various *sicun* can bring:

> A man's medicine bag was hung on a pole outside the lodge and usually brought in at night; it was often "incensed"

with burning sweet grass. It was believed that the presence of the wrong kind of person in the lodge would affect the efficacy of the medicine, and that if it were exposed to such influence for any considerable time its power would be entirely destroyed. (Densmore 252)

Physical health depends on focusing the mind upon a set of symbolic objects, sounds, and actions, which represent the means of continued life. "Bad" or "sick" usually has to do with a loss of concentration, a forgetting of origins. The bear healers remembered the origin of this creation and their participation in it by placing the physical image of the bear in the foreground of their imaginations and at the center of their drama. The performance represents and demonstrates the miracle of sacred transmission which the Lakota never cease to celebrate:

Song of the Bear

minape kin wakan yelo
pezi huta ota yelo

minape kin wakan yelo
taku iyuha ota yelo

My paw is sacred,
herbs are plentiful.

My paw is sacred,
all things are sacred. (Densmore 264)

The singer says "my paw" (not my hand) "is sacred" to acknowledge that he does not permanently possess power but that a power uses his hands and voice to act in the world. The spirit transforms the singer's voice or "paw," a finite part of creation, while the song is sung. A whole person becomes the implementing voice of a particular animal spirit who has compassionately chosen to be audible to those suffering from forgetfulness.

While the song initially heals a wound, the bear *wapiye* eases fear by remembering the abundance of herbs, continually bestowed by the spirits. The people's survival is assured, but to have life, one must be willing to suffer. The singer on the Densmore cylinder groans at the end of each verse to incorporate the one who suffers into the potencies of the remedial song. The patient and the doctor, the human being and the spirit, and the separate persons of the *oyate* (people) fuse temporarily into one being, awakened by the harmonious expression of a single voice. Immediately after the fading "groan," the cry for help, the singer's voice rises in volume on the vocables "hiye, hiye," which introduce the next stanza or the next phase of the cure. The indefinite meaning of the vocables at this point is appropriate to the audible answer to the groan, since such help can only come from a mysterious source. When the vocables stop, the vitality flows back into the words, a sensory form filled with strength and meaning, like the patient's reviving body.

"The Song of the Bear" like other healing songs conveys a sense of concentrated strength moving toward expanded recognition. Black Elk's sucking cure follows the same curve. Not surprisingly, his blue man had been an enemy, a source of paralyzing fear before the grandfathers turned him into a helper (*The Sixth Grandfather* 121, 139). Neihardt's perception is typically dualistic, retaining the blue man only as an agent of famine (see *Black Elk Speaks* 32). Black Elk holds a cup of water in one hand as he spears the blue man who is attempting to take refuge in the Missouri river. Water as an emanation of the Thunder beings extends their capacities to destroy and cleanse. Microscopic beings (*mni watu*) that cause sickness, and monsters (*unktehi*) that might devour those who attempt to cross their domain, live in lakes and rivers (Walker, *Lakota Myth* 243). But Wakinyan, the thunder bird, is their mortal enemy, continually striking them with lightning at every opportunity (see E. Deloria, *Teton Myths* 213–14). One creature, however, became Wakinyan's ally in purifying the water of evil beings. Keya, the turtle, was offered immunity from attack and became a benefactor of man (Walker, *Lakota Myth* 243–44). As the turtle was used by Wakinyan, so the blue man who has caused suffering, becomes Black Elk's agent of amelioration: "Just as I took the spear out, the man turned into a turtle . . . Everything that had been dead came back to life and cheered for killing that enemy" (*The Sixth Grandfather* 121–22). The blue man who had been the cause of drought is thereafter associated with water, the primary symbol of adaptability and healthy growth. When he appears in a cup of water, Black Elk's patients are cured.

Neihardt omits Black Elk's emphasis on the meaning of water. Its changing into ice or steam suggests adaptability and endurance in moving from health to sickness and back to health:

> Water is the great power. The water in the wooden cup represented a big lake. When I was conquering the spirit at the head of the Missouri River I was getting power from the water and now I get power from the water the same as then. Everything is dependent on water. If I had not conquered the bad spirit, I would not have had the power. I had conquered the power of the water in conquering this bad spirit. (*The Sixth Grandfather* 123)

But to embody this medicine, Black Elk must be forceful and determined, having been made to perceive its value:

> In this cup I saw a man painted blue and he had a bow and arrow and he was in distress. He wanted to get out of the water and get away, but I was told to drink it down. They said: "make haste and drink your cup of water." I took it and drank the man too. This blue spirit was a fish and I had drunk it down. From this I received strange power and whenever I was conjuring [*wapiya*] I could actually make this blue man come out and swim in the cup of water I used. (The fish represents the power of the water). (*The Sixth Grandfather* 139).

Like a visual, kinetic, or sound symbol, the fish objectifies an invisible effect of communication. That which is in Black Elk, as with the Bear healers, enters into the patient.

In the preceding scene water corresponds to sound. The sweat lodge entrance faces west, toward the source of rain. Water sings upon the rocks as it becomes steam, a mystery heard, felt, and seen. Fools Crow says the steaming rocks diagnose patients in the Lakota language, "and everyone present hears them" (Mails, *Fools Crow* 98). Water is also important in the *yuwipi* ceremony. At its end a bowl of water is passed around. The last person must be sure to finish the water in the bowl after the others have each taken a drink (see Powers, *Yuwipi* 82–83). Drinking the water is the ceremony's unifying resolution. The last man shows respect for the abundance of fear-quenching symbols by not wasting the water. If the symbols are taken for granted, they may be forgotten, and the people will no longer be able to bring the spirits to renew health and life.

When Black Elk wishes to activate the purifying power in his first cure, he drinks water from a cup like that given him by the western spirit, i.e. he draws in a series of observations, concentrated in a sensory form, like a *sicun*. The similar fluidity of sound passes through barriers of individual identity, to transfer health and strength from medicine man to patient:

> Then I drank part of the water and started toward where the sick boy was and I could feel something moving in my chest and I was sure that it was that little blue man and it made a different sound from anything else. Then I stamped the earth four times standing in front of the boy. Then I put my mouth on the pit of the boy's stomach and drew the north wind through him. At the same time the little blue man was also in my mouth, for I could feel him there. I put a piece of white cloth on my mouth and I saw there was blood on it, showing that I had drawn something out of his body. Then I washed my mouth with some of the water of the cup. And I was now sure that I had power. (*The Sixth Grandfather* 239)

Next, Black Elk transfers power directly by sprinkling an herb over the hot water in the cup: "I mixed it up and put some of it in my mouth and blew it over the boy to the four quarters and gave the rest of it to the boy to drink" (*The Sixth Grandfather* 239).

The same cycle of purification and transference through water occurs in the *heyoka* ceremony (see chapter 5). The meat becomes sacred in the boiling pot and the dangerous exercise of purification is assumed by the *heyokas* when they dip the meat out of the water with their bare hands. They then distribute it to the people so that courage and a willingness to sacrifice will enter into them as well. Sun dancers also radiate the virtues their sacrifice has realized. Before the dance begins they lay hands upon the sick (Mails, *Fools Crow* 137; Mails, *Sundancing at Rosebud and Pine Ridge* 108, 144, 173, 216). Their healing power like that of the *heyokas* emerges only in the context of ceremonial sacrifice. They cannot heal without the immediate purification of their sacred acts, unless they also happen to be medicine men or holy men. But a young man who does not ordinarily cure may have this power temporarily through a specific ordeal. In the lesser test of the sweat lodge, the individual person may be healed without acquiring the power to heal.

Healing practice takes into account the conception of a quadripartite human soul. Good Seat, a sacred man born in 1827, told Walker that the *nagi* is a person's guardian. It is an immortal disembodied spirit that protects the *niya,* the embodied soul, before birth and after death: "His *nagi* is not a part of himself. His *nagi* cares for him and warns him of danger and helps him out of difficulties" (*Lakota Belief and Ritual* 71). When the person dies, his *niya* becomes *wanagi.* Then the *nagi* accompanies the *wanagi* to the spirit world into which it may enter only if it has been imprinted with a Lakota identity or "tattoo" (Dorsey 486; Hassrick 323). As long as the *wanagi* is *woniya,* in the body, it may be strengthened in the sweat lodge "where they make vitality" (*inikagapi*). Another soul, the *nagila,* distinguishes the human species from other forms of life and relates the person to these forms. The *nagila* maintains the involuntary physical processes of the body as a kind of vegetable soul. Finally, the *sicun* is a quality of strength characterizing each individual (Walker, *Lakota Belief and Ritual* 70–73; Amiotte 26–32).

Just as a particular power could be maintained in a physical object and thereby become a *sicun,* so in this sense, the human body holding particular abilities may be similarly conceived. While all people were born holding one *sicun* in their bodies, more could be acquired in fasts and vision quests. Frank Fools Crow, as mentioned, was able to acquire the *sicun* of all 405 Lakota spirits. Black Elk too had numerous spirit helpers and so was able to cure in every mode of Lakota medicine, while most healers were empowered by only one or two spirits (see *The Sixth Grandfather* 84, 86).

Black Elk's incorporation of multiple *sicun* has bearing on the many-in-one concept of Wakan Tanka. Some missionaries have insisted that the Lakota were chaotic polytheists and therefore needed to know a "higher" omnipotence (see Steinmetz 39–44). In the 1850s Lynd observed that "no one deity" was "a superior object of worship," and Pond discredited reports of belief in "a supreme existence called the Great Spirit" (Dorsey 432). But Sword told Walker of a Wakan Tanka contemplated best in his physical manifestations but never directly seen:

> Wakan Tanka is like sixteen different persons; but each person is *kan* [sacred]. Therefore, they are all only the same as one . . . All the God persons have *ton*. The *ton* is the power to do supernatural things . . . Half of the Good Gods have *tan ton* (have physical properties), and half are *tan ton śni* (have no physical properties). Half of those who are *tan ton* are *tan ton yan* (visible) and half of those who are *tan ton śni* are *tan ton yan śni* (invisible). All the other Gods are visible or invisible as they choose to be. (*Lakota Belief and Ritual* 95; see also Hassrick 245)

This balance of invisibility and visibility conveys a sense of transient forms infused with hidden, unifying power. Instead of a triune godhead many Lakota have long conceived of a deity with innumerable faces, like Brahman or the ten thousand things of Taoism: "The Sioux . . . had always believed in a mysterious power whose greatest manifestation is the sun, and that Wakan Tanka was the manifestation of that power" (Densmore 85). Black Elk consistently expresses the many-in-one view of Wakan Tanka offered to Walker by Little Wound: "The Wakan Tanka are those which made everything . . . Wakan Tanka are many. But they are all the same as one" (*Lakota Belief and Ritual* 70; see also 73, 95, 99).

The continual appearance of the invisible in relative rather than absolute forms characterizes the Lakota oral tradition. Instead of adhering to fixed scriptures, narrators like Black Elk conveyed their formative purpose in improvised words, producing stories that were similar, like members of a species, but never identical, never unfolding the same way twice. Events, deeds, and their doers were interchangeable. In one Stone Boy story, the hero may resemble the noble Falling Star, in another he plays tricks with Iktomi (see Allison). Each narrator had a parflèche of ingredients to arrange as the spirits moved him.

This emphasis on variable forms for the same spirit occurs in a mid-nineteenth century report of Dakota belief in reincarnation. Gideon Pond, like his brother, Samuel (see chapter 5 and conclusion), a missionary to the Minnesota Sioux, described their "superstitions" for Schoolcraft in 1857 and again for the Minnesota Historical Society in 1867. Despite his contempt for the magicians he sought to expose, he unintentionally (providentially?) illuminated a significant Lakota belief.

Pond's informants told of the spiritual evolution of a *wicaśa wakan:* "The original essence of these men and women, for they appear under both sexes, first wakes into existence floating in ether. As the winged seed of the thistle, or of the cottonwood, floats on the air, so they are gently wafted by the 'four winds'— 'Takuśkanśkan'" to the gods who welcome them "into intimate fellowship" (G. Pond 49; see also Dorsey 494). There the "embryotic" *wakan* man is taught "all the chants, feasts, fasts, dances, and sacrificial rites which it is deemed necessary to impose on men" (G. Pond 49; Dorsey 494).

His powers of healing, discovering "things concealed from common men," and foretelling future events, are then enumerated, and it is with these potentialities that the soul of the medicine man enters the body of the new born infant. Perhaps this is another way of expressing the receptiveness of Lakota spiritual experience. Without the entrance of spirits into a ceremonial circle, the physical beings present cannot be animated to fulfill and renew the world. The spirits, like the souls of the medicine man, are thought to come from somewhere else, from potentiality into visible form. When the spirit leaves and the medicine man dies, he returns to the "abode of his gods," as Pond puts it, "where he receives a new inspiration and a new commission, to serve a new generation of men in some other portion of the world" (G. Pond 50; Dorsey 494).

The cycle of spiritual growth becomes complete in the representative number of "four inspirations and incarnations" after which the medicine man "returns to his primitive nothingness." The cycle Pond describes resembles the Buddhist concept of nirvana. And although other texts exclude reincarnation, the emergence of a world of myriad forms from a mystery into which the forms return is consistent in Lakota expression. Pond adds that these *wakan* spirits can take the forms of the wolf, bear, buffalo, and other animals. This too is consistent with the Lakota sense of spiritual wisdom emerging through many *akicita* (messengers). Reincarnation as an animal is not a punishment or a result of bad karma.

Powers has advanced a theory that the four Lakota souls— *nagi, niya, nagila,* and *sicun*—represent a diachronic development rather than a structural differentiation: "The terms are tied together as parts of a descriptive process that demark stages in the coming-into-being-and-dying process of each individual" (*Sacred Language* 135). He adds that the potentiality of creation is fulfilled in *nagi* and that the other souls are stages in a series of spiritual incarnations in an individual life: "when we look at their interrelationships and dynamic quality, the parts blend neatly into an interpretation which emphasizes the whole life process as one in which immortality is achieved through reincarnation." And he sees the number four as the "unfolding, the development, the evolution of important events" (Powers, *Sacred Language* 136).

Pete Catches has said that the Lakota believe in reincarnation but the details are known only to holy men and cannot be told to outsiders (conversation with the author in Pine Ridge, South Dakota, July 1984). Some contemporary Lakota do not think that their people ever believed in reincarnation. Perhaps Good Seat's definition of *nagi* and *wanagi* allows us to glimpse at least one older Lakota conception. *Nagi* is the synchronic life of Lakota culture, while *woniya* is its individual embodiment. In his Great Vision Black Elk's *nagi* is revealed to him by the western grandfather: "Take courage and be not afraid, for you will know him. And furthermore, behold him, whom you shall represent. By representing him, you shall be very powerful on earth in medicines and all powers. He is your spirit and you are his body and his name is Eagle Wing Stretches" (*The Sixth Grandfather* 116). While Eagle Wing Stretches may take many bodies, Black Elk comes to know himself as his transient but indispensable helper.

SEVEN

Becoming a Helper

BLACK ELK's autobiography reveals a developmental pattern, from the helplessness of a sick child to the spiritual potency of a young man whose story ends in marriage, a significant culmination omitted by Neihardt. The growth of Black Elk's consciousness may be something like Powers's suggested outline. Black Elk incorporates the various potentialities of human existence until he reincarnates Eagle Wing Stretches. Corresponding social acts reflect this spiritual development. When a young man has sufficiently extended his visionary awareness, he is ready to take a wife. Without supernatural assistance, no man would be capable of feeding or defending a family.

As the two representative oral narratives to be discussed here will show, the most accomplished warrior or spiritual seeker is never without an ally even when he is physically alone. Though Black Elk's Great Vision comes unsought, the first deeply significant event in most men's lives is *hanbleceya* (the crying-for-a-dream or vision quest ritual), during which he is "pitied" by the invisible being who helps him discover his particular gifts. Black Elk's *hanbleceya* results in his Dog vision (*The Sixth Grandfather* 227–32) and augments the Thunder powers received in his first vision. The rite achieves part of its purpose in its condition of absolute isolation from human contact. While fasting and praying for three to four days and nights on top of a mountain, the vision-seeker maintains alertness for a sign from his sought companion (see Black Elk's description in *The Sacred Pipe* 44–66).

Many Lakota stories send their protagonists into ordeals re-sembling *hanbleceya*. Once having gained a spirit-guide, the hero in succeeding adventures or other stories acquires a group of guardian spirits whom he may evoke whenever he is faced with difficulty. Crazy Horse had a sacred stone the use of which he learned from the Thunder beings in one of his visions. He rubbed it all over his body before going into battle to make himself bullet and arrow-proof. He would then run a buckskin thong through a hole in the stone and hang it around his neck so that the stone would cover his heart. He was never wounded but the power of this stone was reinforced by other rites:

> Occasionally he carried a little medicine bag, which he also fastened around his neck. From the bag he would take a small portion of the dried heart and brain of an eagle mixed with dried wild aster flowers. This mixture he would chew, also using some of it to rub on his body. Sometimes Crazy Horse would apply dirt thrown up by the burrowing blind mole to his horse in lines and streaks—not painting him with the dirt, but passing it over him in a certain way with his hands, touching a little of it to his own hair with the addition of two or three short straws of grass. This would render horse and rider invisible and invulnerable to bullets and arrows. (Kadlecek 13; see also Black Elk's reference to Crazy Horse's stone, *The Sixth Grandfather* 203–4)

The protective power was often transferred through a meto-nymic animal part, representing some obvious virtue such as the mole's invisibility. But burrowing animals also represented the overall process of spiritual manifestation as beings who knew two worlds, like the vision-seeker who entered into the spirit world to receive spiritual power; moles, wolves, coyotes, and others brought pure earth from underground, as uncontami-nated as the previously hidden wisdom brought into visibility by the *wamakaśkan* (spirit animals) who answer prayers for wisdom and efficacy. Mole earth was preferred for sacred rituals since it foreshadowed the appearance of something curative (Powers 57). Ants were also reputed to bring something pure into human perception and Crazy Horse dreamed of ants as well: "he grabbed ant hill dirt and threw it to the four winds for protection in battle" (Kadlecek 150).

Crazy Horse was known for the extraordinary spiritual power that protected him in battle. Other warriors like White Bull relied more on their physical prowess and practical experience, although White Bull too received warrior powers in visions of the thunders, the elk, and the buffalo (Vestal, *Warpath* xv). Virtually all young Lakota men had acquired at least one helper before they went on their first war party. George Bushotter describes the effect of summoning a helper in the midst of battle: "No matter how severe is his opponent, that opponent grows instantly weak, they say, when the guardian spirit of the Dakota is remembered by him, and called; for he then acts for his master. Then the Dakota can treat his enemy badly" (E. Deloria, *Teton Myths* 245:1).

Like Crazy Horse, Black Elk was a Thunder dreamer, and in his only mature opportunity to act as a warrior, immediately after Wounded Knee, he too puts dirt all over himself (*The Sixth Grandfather* 277) and depends specifically for protection upon the northern spirits of his vision, even though his general power, especially for healing comes from the west: "Then I recalled my vision, the north where the geese were; then I outstretched my hands [and my rifle] and then made the goose sound. They pumped away at me from the creek then, but not a single bullet came near me—they couldn't hit me" (277). When he briefly forgets to sound the cry in the heat of battle, he is seriously wounded: "I should have gone right on imitating the goose with my power and I would have been bullet-proof. My doubt and my fear for the moment killed my power and during that moment I was shot" (277–78).

Physical combat was not the only place to which a helper might be summoned. The Lakota young men could encounter domestic frustrations sent by trickster spirits more detrimental to the spiritual wholeness of the nation than the socially unifying threat of enemy tribes. The first story in *Teton Myths*, the George Bushotter collection, translated by Ella Deloria, is entitled "The Myth of Miwakan Yuhala" 'Sword Owner,' and it

epitomizes the pattern of a young man's most difficult encoun-
ters in and out of the camp circle. Many stories begin with the
hero living just beyond the circle with a grandmother or other
isolated guardian, much as Black Elk is initially isolated by sickness. People live "outside" when they are unable to contribute
fully to the group's sustenance (E. Deloria, *Dakota Texts* 112n).
Although most children live physically within the circle, boys
do not really participate in the life of the nation until they feed
and defend it. They are in the circle when they are very young
but they do not maintain it. The Lakota oral narratives define a
person on the basis of what he or she does rather than on the
basis of their characteristics. Few adjectives are used to describe
people. In the stories a person becomes a model of Lakota being
without benefit of editorial praise. Persuasive charm is for tricksters, but power is made plain in action.

The condition of the hero at the beginning is often "wild" or
unformed. His living without a full network of relatives around
him symbolizes the isolated egotism of a child, and he soon reveals an instinct to grow into those relationships by conceiving
and expressing them with clarity. The child begins with a vague
assurance of simple protection by various members of his extended family who, being initially undifferentiated, are nar-
ratively reduced to one or two, usually a grandmother, in this
case a father and an older brother. The father represents the
young man's physical security but his "second father," his older
brother, has supernatural power and helps the boy, like a guiding spirit in a vision, when he is ready to become a man:

> Heces wanna wicaśa wan cinca nunpa can makośkanl ti
> keyapi. Tokapa ki he Miwakan-Yuhala eciyapi na śunkaku
> ki Hakela eciyapi śke.

> And so now there was a man who with his two sons lived
> out alone, in a solitary place. The elder was called Sword-
> Owner, and the younger was Hakela (Last Born). (E. De-
> loria, *Teton Myths* 1, 20).[1]

---

1. With the exception of direct quotations from *Teton Myths* and *Dakota
Texts,* the Lakota language in this book is written according to the Buechel

Hakela wishes to become part of the *wicoti* (tribal encampment) but to do so he must travel over territory physically and spiritually dangerous, and therefore his brother imparts the means of survival. As Bushotter mentions, in describing the protection of guardian-spirits, a man must have the presence of mind to "remember" his source of power in a crisis. "Kiksuya" 'remember' is an especially important Lakota word in prayer as well. To remember a spirit means to know its presence in an enhanced alertness, and strength, to be inhabited as it were by an extraordinary feeling of resourcefulness wherever and whenever that may be required. In the last of his Ghost Dance visions, the Thunders remind Black Elk of his only real means of helping the people: "toward the west I saw a flaming rainbow that I had seen in the first vision. On either side of this rainbow was a cloud and right above me there was an eagle soaring, and he said to me: 'Behold them, the Thunder-being nation, you are relative-like to them. Hence, remember this'" (*The Sixth Grandfather* 265).

A supernatural spirit, received by a man who remembers it in formal prayer or in the midst of a crisis, watches over that man like an older relative may literally have watched over him as a child. Black Elk's protectors are "grandfathers," but other terms of address were also used. In prayers and stories names like "tunkaśila" 'grandfather' or "ciye" 'older brother' do not

---

system as set down in his *Dictionary of the Teton Dakota Sioux Language* (Pine Ridge, South Dakota: Red Cloud Indian School, 1970). The phonetic symbols used here are essential and minimal. Lakota orthography can be complex, but I have assumed that most non-English sounds will be automatically understood by speakers and readers of Lakota. Clear and significant differences of meaning are attached to words with *s* as opposed to *ś* (pronounced "sh"). The same is true for words with *h* rather than *ḣ* (gutteral, as in "Bach" but softer). Ella Deloria's orthography differs considerably from Buechel's. I have applied Buechel's orthography to passages from *Teton Myths* and *Dakota Texts*, but I have not generally changed her spelling. A notable exception occurs in the writing of the nasalized *n* which Buechel writes as ŋ and Deloria writes as a subscript hook under the preceding letter. Thus Deloria spells "wolf" *suŋkmanitu*, while Buechel spells it *suŋkmanitu*. The common modern practice, such as that used by DeMallie in *The Sixth Grandfather*, is to print ŋ simply as *n, sunkmanitu*.

necessarily mean an immediate relative in the Euro-American sense. Relational terms applied to the spirits express feelings of trust but also enhanced respect and care not to offend. In this story the relational term for a guiding spirit is "ciye," since Hakela is helped by his literal "ciye":

> Tohanl wanna letanhan ilanin na tuktel taku teȟika wanji ayakipa kinhan miyeksuyin na leȟinkta ce: "Ciye Miwakan Yuhala," ehinkta lo; kinhan hecegla tuktel yau ki hel wan-mayatakin kte lo. Nakun misun le iwaktaya omayani yo.

> Upon leaving this place you will go along; and when you meet with trouble somewhere, you must remember me and say, "Elder brother Sword-Owner" and straightway you shall see me there where you are. Moreover, my younger brother, be on your guard about this as you travel. (E. Deloria, *Teton Myths* 1, 20)

The first cautionary statement, made by Sword-Owner and simultaneously by the narrator, is made with the understanding that initially it will fail to be heeded. Hakela is instructed to remain on the road to "the tribal encampment" to find his place among the people. This ought to be the centered purpose of a young man's life, but a young man is especially vulnerable to diverting trickery from a significantly generalized "tuwa" 'someone' who will cause Hakela to take the wrong path and "meet with misfortune." At the same time that this prophecy of suffering is unreservedly hard, Hakela's survival is absolutely assured by the ubiquity of his *ciye* who "owns" the means of deliverance: "'Tokša tohanl woteȟi ayakipa kinhan henaȟci wan-mayalakinkta ce,' eciye" "'I promise you that there you thus meet with misfortune, right at that very place, you shall see me," he said to him' (E. Deloria, *Teton Myths* 1, 20).

Hakela departs, and the expected "someone" tempts him to leave the road and to believe that the wisdom of his elders is a lie. Hakela's identity here is collective, as his name suggests. Individuals may be lost, but in each generation Lakota boys will find their way to manhood. When Hakela leaves the sustaining foundation of *Lakol wicoh'an* (Lakota ways) the earth divides beneath his feet and he is left crying within a deep crevice. But as soon as Hakela remembers to "remember" (E. Deloria, *Speaking of Indians* 40) his "older brother" appears: "na wancak miwakan kin un maka el ape" 'and with his magic blade, the sword, he struck the earth' (E. Deloria, *Teton Myths* 2–3, 21). Hakela then instantly rises to a more advanced level, and no longer trapped in fear and helplessness, he finds himself standing on top of the hill next to his *ciye*.

Hakela's first lesson has taught him to be humble in relation to the powers upon which he needs to rely. He is now mature enough to wield power in a material form. The older brother makes him a "sword-owner," one who carries medicine to defend the people. Hakela now possesses the warrior's ability to summon power by means of a spiritual object in a ritual which he personally "owns." And as Crazy Horse had several symbolic means of defense, and as Black Elk used his sacred bow and his goose cry after Wounded Knee (*The Sixth Grandfather* 274, 277), so now Hakela symbolically grows in potency as his means of power increase. In addition to his sword, Sword-Owner gives Hakela a quiver to hold the potencies or *sicun* (Walker, *Lakota Belief and Ritual* 95–96), which human beings can ceremonially transfer to objects:

> Na ciyeku ki heciye: "Misun, miwakan ki le un takuke ceyaś yaktekta ce," eyin; "na wahinkpe ki hena un taku kinyan un ki yaokta lo," eye.

> The elder brother said: "My brother, with the sword you can kill anything at all, and with the arrows you can hit whatever lives by flying." (E. Deloria, *Teton Myths* 3, 21)

(Black Elk's power to kill is in his Thunder spear that flashes lightning when he stabs the blue man, *The Sixth Grandfather* 121). Hakela now has the power to subdue danger on the earth and in the "other" world of the sky. By killing the red eagle later in the story Hakela acquires the solar potency to give and sustain life.

Proceeding again on his own Hakela is ready to subdue residual childhood fears of being alone and of being mistreated by strangers. In a thickly wooded place on a dark night Hakela hears the occasional cry of a child, which shakes his confidence because he is only a few years from crying himself. But this time he immediately remembers his power:

> "Ciye miwakan ki le un takuni ohowalakteśni keye un, ito takpe-bla yanke," ecin. Ho heces wanna etkiya inazinzin yahe. Yunkan wanna ikiyela ye icunhan Anuk-Ite ki heca wan tankalahcaka hinazin na hokśicala wan uśika ite ki ataya śayela yuh eyayapi ca yuha nazin na tohanl ceyeśni ca uzizitkahu ki heca wan un ite-opta iyuheyaya can lila ceye.

> "For didn't my elder brother say this blade would keep me from having to yield to anything? I think I shall go forth to meet, to fight this thing." With that he started ahead, albeit he halted from time to time as he advanced. He came to a Double-face of giant size, who stood there holding a poor child, its face streaked red with scratches. Each time it stopped crying, he took some thorny stalks of the wild rose, and drew them across its face so that it cried loudly again. (Deloria, *Teton Myths* 3–4, 21–22)

The narrator indicates that overcoming one's own barely outgrown fear is no easy task. Hakela presses forward to see an image of childish impotence, exactly the image that Lakota children were raised to overcome. Games, the participation of children in rituals, the extensive "honoring" of children, the avoidance of repressive or corporal discipline developed a temperament of adventurousness and independence (Hassrick 315–25). Black Elk's extensive descriptions of child rearing and games in particular bear this out (*The Sixth Grandfather* 106–7, 148–49, 323–25).

Not surprisingly then, the spirit-dulling monster soothes the child as much as it torments him. Even benevolence can be monstrous if it creates helplessness. Hakela's independence is newly won. He is on the way to join the people, to become an adult. The Double-Face, an intentionally vague monster

(Deloria, *Dakota Texts* 50n) epitomizing many forms of evil, threatens to reduce Hakela to infantile panic:

> Na wanna etkiya yin na ihukuya inazin. Yunkan Anuk-Ite heye: "Niś eya kakiś-ciya yacin na el mayau he?" eya tkaś Hakela iś ayuptin na heye: "Hiya, niyeś pa ki ḣmuyela kaksa iyeciyinkta ca el ciha yelo."

> So he went to him, and stood at his feet (literally under him). And the Double-face asked, "Do you come to me so that I may abuse you also?" But Hakela replied, "O no, I come to strike off your head and send it humming." (Deloria, *Teton Myths* 3–4, 22)

In Lakota culture evil is often identified by its humming sound, "ḣmu" (Deloria, *Dakota Texts* 145, 158). The vibrations can immobilize a potential victim with fear. But the expressions of evil are crudely brutal and can be silenced by the articulation of a keener virtue. Several *wicaḣmunga,* men who are allied to evil spirits, do not dare to disrupt Black Elk's Buffalo ceremony with *ḣmu* because they know his "power is very great" (*The Sixth Grandfather* 241).

In this universal confrontation Hakela now assumes the role of *ciye* himself to effect an explicitly psychological deliverance. Hakela and the child arrive at the lodge of the child's parents who are so old that they can barely see. The parents rejoice at the child's return and serve a meal, after which everyone lies down to sleep. Again, the threat to independence and courage is posed but this time from potential regression into coziness and unwary security. As *ciye,* Hakela must help his younger brother to grow away from the overprotectiveness of "blind" parents:

> Yunkan wanna woligluśtanpi ca kul yunahinna heye: "Ina, misun hiyuyi ye, ito yuha munkelakte" eya tka "Hiya, ceye s'a ca hanhepi ataya ni yukakizinkte," eye. Tka "Hiya, hececa keyaś hiyuyi ye, ina," eya canke wanna iyekiyapi. Yunkan iyehankecaiciya yuśtan.

> And after the meal, he lay down, and said, "Mother, let me take my little brother and sleep with him." But she replied,

"No it won't do; he cries so much, he will annoy you all night." But, "That doesn't matter, just let me take him, mother," he insisted, so they passed the child over to him. And all night long he spent stretching it till morning. By then he made him the same height as himself. (Deloria, *Teton Myths* 5–6, 23)

In the morning the old man's response to this miracle is humorous and yet thematically serious: "Winunhca, kikta yo! Micinkśi wiinahma agli yelo" 'Wife, get up! My son has brought home a woman!' A young man who brings home a woman is no longer a child but at the same time Hakela is ensuring that his younger brother will not *be* a woman (see Hassrick 133 on the *winkte* [transvestite] as a victim of parental overprotection). Before he leaves, he gives the spirit-sword to the former child who must proceed in his own "story" to become himself and to transmit his power.

The end of Black Elk's story in the transcript follows the conventions of Lakota oral narrative. He proves himself in battle after Wounded Knee and ends the autobiographical section with the words: "Two years later I was married" (*The Sixth Grandfather* 282). Having proved his courage, Hakela too "arrives" at the camp circle as one who can sustain it. The Chief's daughter is promised to the one who shoots down any one of a group of eagles circling above the tribal circle. Eagles fly very high, usually beyond the reach of even a powerful bow. If Hakela can bring one down, he will be impervious to the petty jealousies and wasteful rivalries that can destroy a man in the circle, even one who has confronted many enemies on the outside. Hakela shoots down a red eagle, a recurrent motif in the oral narratives (E. Deloria, *Dakota Texts* 112), and gains the red virtues of the sun and the buffalo for the harmonious marriage he seeks.

The eagle's peculiar fall is emphasized: "kutkiya pemnimni s'e u na hinhpaye" 'downward it fell, appearing to be twisted, as it came, revolving in the fall' (E. Deloria, *Teton Myths* 6, 23). Although Hakela does lose his own power in subsequent events, he must undergo a transformation that is like an extended fall. From the freedom a warrior feels outside the circle, he must descend to the ensnaring social conflicts that divisively threaten the nation. At first Hakela knows only the glory of a young hero. The people carry him to the chief's lodge on a white buffalo robe, but the chief's eldest daughter refuses to marry him because he is not handsome enough. Then, as if to mitigate this unlooked for humiliation the chief's second daughter agrees to accept him.

Nevertheless, in the confusing world of the camp circle, matters are not so easily resolved as when stealing horses or counting coup. Attractiveness is shifting and relative. When Hakela is unpredictably transformed into a handsome man by a "feather ornament," something that typically causes people to perceive a man as desirable, the older sister has fits of regret but cannot get her younger sister to surrender her prize. The relationship of the sisters contrasts sharply here to the relationship between Hakela and Sword-Owner earlier:

> "Mitan, unśimakila na wicaśa tokiyopeunkiciyinkte" eya, tkaś ecanl ihaha na heye: "He toka ekta nici yeś waḣiteyalaśni k'un, he toka ca nake hehan he?" eya.

> "Younger sister, let us exchange husbands," but instead the other laughed scornfully, saying, "That one desired you at the beginning but you despised him, why the sudden change which makes you propose that?" (E. Deloria, *Teton Myths* 7, 24)

People must learn to accept their individual attributes and those of their companions, and to contribute to the nation's strength rather than weakening it by wishing to surpass others within the circle. The eldest sister steals Hakela's feather ornament and places it on the head of her own husband who immediately becomes very handsome. But the story's listeners represent those who can see through an unearned reputation. They know Hakela's true identity, even when he ostensibly turns into a dog and is kicked out of the tipi by the older sister, to the chagrin and sorrow of his wife. Hakela has earned his place as a man of the circle by his prior deeds, which are unaffected by metamorphoses of physical and social perception. These deeds

have "spoken" the story into being and have irrefutably defined
Hakela's manhood, like the coups transformed into words by
a returned warrior and formally borne witness to by fellow
warriors (Hassrick 33). Hakela's brother-in-law is only an un-
developed image who has not exercised the prerogatives of
maleness. Hakela, on the other hand, has given the people courage by killing the Double-Face and self-esteem by shooting
down the red eagles. He has acted as a mature adult by transmitting power to the boy he rescued. Now he continues to provide
food without reward and without empty praise. Most impor-
tantly he "tells" a story that sharpens the people's vision and recalls them to their true selves.

At first the message seems like incomprehensible "whining,"
when the "dog" tries to recall the wife to their true purpose of
feeding others. The girl decides to "follow" the dog as the listeners should follow the story. The "matter" of the story lies in
what she discovers: "Yunkan lece capa wan kte na heyata aglig-
nakin na heyahan" 'and this is what was the matter: The dog had
killed a beaver and dragged it away from the water and had been
saying that, trying to tell her' (E. Deloria, *Teton Myths* 8, 24).
The narrator tells us to overcome egotism and its resultant despair by seeing ourselves as our deeds. Individuals need not
measure themselves against others if they act consistently to
give life to all. Those who live on vanity will end up with nothing to make themselves strong. As the daughter "spoke to
them," at the end, the narrator has spoken throughout:

> "Wicaśa-waśte hignayan keyin na takuni okihiśni ikce waś-
> teicila kul yunkahe ceyaś tohanl śunka-mitawa ki taku kte ki
> tohanl he esa luhapin kte śni ye" ewicakiye.

> "You say you have married a handsome man, but he can do
> nothing but lie about, being very fond of himself; but
> when my dog kills something, you shall have none of it,
> not even the hide." So she spoke to them. (E. Deloria,
> *Teton Myths* 8, 24)

A man becomes strong that the people may live. Hakela progresses from heroic deeds to an identity that seems contemp-

tible to the immature, but in terms of the Lakota values established in the story he fills an indispensable role in the camp he had wished to join from the beginning of his journey. The worst disgrace is to be useless, to be a parasite. But the "dog" who hunts well becomes the wolf who will lead his *misun* (younger brothers) outside the camp circle where they become men. Hakela can "stretch" others with the story of his life, especially the last part, which is at first unintelligible to less advanced listeners—the younger sister thinks he is whining. The story's message can only be remembered as medicine when the listeners learn to hear. While a dog is considered sacred only in special circumstances, such as the *heyoka* ceremony, Black Elk told Neihardt two stories of how dogs saved human beings who heeded their "speech" (*The Sixth Grandfather* 357–60).

At the beginning Hakela could not remember how to walk toward the people. At the end he remembers who he is and what he is for. Not only does he not fear helplessness, he does not fear a lessened self-esteem imposed by rivals. He has attained his full height, his full capacity for unselfish usefulness. Perhaps Hakela's humility helps to explain Black Elk's willingness to assume a mantle of Christianity and to apparently compromise his own beliefs. As a *heyoka* he had displayed a ludicrous persona, like Hakela's canine one, in order to "save" others. As a Christian, Black Elk may have put his relatives before ritual forms. His original religion had existed only for the people. Lakota religious practices were freely revised (Walker, *Lakota Belief* 25–26), and baptism may have precipitated a change of image and a new name (Nicholas), while Eagle Wing Stretches remained protectively alert.

In "Hokśila Wan" 'A Boy' in Buechel's *Lakota Tales and Texts* another Hakela receives supernatural assistance from a relative to effect rescue from a Double-Face. In general resemblance to the widely told "Inyan Hokśila" 'Stone Boy' (see Jahner, "Stone Boy: Persistent Hero" 175) three older brothers have successively gone off to look for missing people and none have returned. As the remaining brother laments because he is too young to hunt for his mother, an unknown woman arrives. She addresses him as "misun" 'younger brother,' and he in turn brings her to stand politely outside his mother's *tipi* where the making of relatives proceeds: "Hunku kin okiyaka na wana 'Ina, cunkśiya yo; tankewayelo,' eya" 'He spoke to his mother and now, "Mother, make yourself a daughter; I have made her my older sister," he said' (Buechel, *Lakota Tales and Texts* 374). The new daughter and sister is later revealed to have come from the buffalo nation, a power predominant in protecting the family (see Walker, *Sun Dance* 84, and chapter 9).

Her first lesson (and that of the narrator) demonstrates the purposeful use of symbols. As she provides physical defense, so her exact verbal repetition secures a complete circle: "'Misun, wahinkpe topa ka kaksa ye . . . Yunkan wanji śaya ye,' eya, 'na wanji toya ye,' eya, 'na wanji sabya ye,' eya, 'na wanji giya ye,' eya" '"Younger brother, cut four arrows . . . Then make one red," she said, "and make one blue," she said, "and make one black," she said, "and make one brown," she said' (Buechel, *Lakota Tales and Texts* 375). In addition to the arrows and the magical words that will remain in his memory, the young woman gives him a medicine, like the eagle heart used by Crazy Horse, to chew and rub on his body before confronting danger. When Hakela comes to the Double-Face in the midst of his afternoon slumber, he is to blow the medicine on the arrows before driving them into the monster's head. Then he must cut into the enormous belly and draw out his brothers: "'Heci mahel niunpi ca tokśa wanwicalakin kte,' eya" '"And so they are alive inside and soon you will see them," she said' (Buechel, *Lakota Tales and Texts* 375; cf. E. Deloria, *Dakota Texts* 1–8).

In the same way the woman draws Hakela out of amorphous fear and into the clear reality of distinct relationships. Following a sweat lodge ceremony (used to cleanse departing warriors, see *The Sacred Pipe* 54), she blows some of the medicine on him before fastening the rest to his scalp lock, the passage through which his *niya* (breath of life) enters and leaves his body. This medicine will "awanyankin kte" 'watch over him' and instruct him so that he cannot make a mistake. On the first night of his journey, Hakela's helper yanks his top knot, waking him up in the middle of the night and again at dawn to demonstrate his constant guard. (Cf. Black Elk's hearing a voice say, "raise your head," just in time for he and his uncle to escape discovery by sixty enemy warriors, *The Sixth Grandfather* 205).

The duration of the journey is then suggested in patterns of exact verbal repetition, since Hakela's intervening travel and growth are as important to the story as his heroic achievement. (Buechel's prose transcription is here put into poetic lines in order to highlight the narrator's typically Lakota phrasing):

> Na wana iyaya;
> na wana anpetu ataya ya,
> na hanhepi ca paha wan el iwanka;
> na hancokanyan hehan
> tuwa pecokan el yuzi
> na "Kikta yo," eya
> ca el etonwe,
> eyaś tuweni śni;
> na ake iyunka.
> Yunkan wana anpo kta itokab
> ake tuwa pecokan el yuzi
> na "wana anpa ye; kikta yo," eya.
> Hecel hehanl pejuta wan pegnake k'un he e ca slolya.
> Na wana inajin na ya.
> Na ake hanhepi,
> tka paha akanl iyunka.
> Yunkan ake econ
> na anpa el ake econ.
> Hecel ake inajin na ya.
> Na hanhepi
> el paha wan akanl iyunka.
> Na ake econ
> na ake anpa el econ.
> Hecel inajin na ya.
> Na wana ake ħtayetu iwanka.
> Na ake econ.
> Hecel ake inajin na ya
> na ħe wan lila tanka ca el ihunni.
> Ehanl oiyokpaza.
> Hecel hel iwanka.

Yunkan wana hancokanyan el econ na.
Na wana anpa hehanl lecel eya:
"Wana wicole le kin le kuta paha wan ska
ca pestola ca yanke kin hel oȟlateya iśtinmin kta
ca paha kin el aśnikiyi na tohanl ciyugice kin el ya yo," eya.
Hece inajin na wana iyaya.
Na paha wan eya k'un he el ihunni.
Yunkan he lila tanka na wankatuya. (Buechel, *Lakota Tales and
    Texts* 375–76)

And now he set out;
and now all day he traveled,
and [slept at] night on top of a hill;
and then in the middle of the night
someone pulled his top knot
and "wake up," it said,
so he looked,
but there was no one there,
and again he lay down.
And then just before dawn,
again someone pulled his top knot
and "now it is dawn; wake up," it said.
And so from then on he knew that it was the medicine
    fastened in his hair.
And now he arose and traveled.
And again it was night,
so he lay down on top of a hill.
Then again [the medicine] did that.
And again at dawn it did that.
And so again he arose and traveled.
And again it was night
so he lay down on top of a hill.
And again [the medicine] did that.
And again at dawn it did that.
And so he arose and traveled.
And now again at evening [he lay] on top [of a hill].
And again [the medicine] did that.
And so again he arose and traveled,
and he came to a very big mountain.

107

Then it was twilight.
And so he [went] to the top.
Then in the middle of the night [the medicine] did that again.
And now at dawn it spoke like this:
"Now the one you are seeking is at the bottom of a white
  [snowcapped] mountain.
So lay a sharpened stick next to you while you sleep,
and when I wake you on the hill, then go," it said.
And so he arose and traveled.
And he came to that mountain, the one spoken of,
And it was very large and high. (My translation)

In the immediate vicinity of the monster Hakela hears the buzzing sound that announces an evil spirit. But *himu* cannot harm those whose ears are attuned to distinct instructions for prayer and action. The medicine near his *niya* tells Hakela that evil is vulnerable because its scope is so limited—it often "sleeps." The speaking medicine and the narrator offer the same warning: "'wanna el yi na iśtinma . . . inahni yo'" '"now go on in while he is sleeping . . . hurry"' (Buechel, *Lakota Tales and Texts* 376). The rescue mission then progresses beyond dramatic deliverance, and Hakela's being helped, to Hakela's becoming the helper. After telling his brothers that they must kill four buffalo before they can go home, he uses his medicine to make them invisible, teaching them to connect humility and effectiveness. By ritually eating the raw meat they gather strength to soothe those who wait rather than demanding solace themselves.

A cycle of prosperity then begins, and again events that are undramatic are not considered trivial. Hakela is made an *itancan* (leader) and finds a wife with whom he and his sister live in harmony. A child is born and shortly after that Hakela is honored with a name, "Mahpiya Wakan" 'Sacred Cloud.' Then his sister announces her intent to take a journey. This will be a temporary departure but it foreshadows her final return to the spirit world at the end of this story. The first journey is a transition, as if to accustom Mahpiya Wakan to carry his responsibilities without her immediate presence. Like the most *wakan* buffalo woman to

ever visit the tribe, the sister of Maḣpiya Wakan is also a sister to
the people (see Densmore 65).

The Lakota brother-sister relationship is a particularly re-
vered expression of respect. In George Sword's story of the establishment of the directions, Yata who eventually becomes the
North, expresses his characteristic crudity when he refuses to
accept Woḣpe, the daughter of Škan, as a sister rather than a
wife (Walker, *Lakota Myth* 202), and in Black Elk's 1944 story,
"Pouting Butte," a young man becomes suicidal when his sister
scolds him (*The Sixth Grandfather* 341–42). The Lakota derived
an ideal of loyalty from the brother-sister bond, and they extended it to all friendly relations. Brothers and sisters loved each
other unconditionally without distrust or fear of loss: "The high
respect . . . continued throughout life and was constantly reinforced by acts of generosity and signs of affection. It was for
her brother, not her husband, that a women made moccasins.
And a brother, by the same token, brought scalps honoring his
mother and sister, not his wife" (Hassrick 109).

Even after the buffalo woman in "Hokšila Wan" returns to
the buffalo nation, she will continue to be a sister, sister-in-law,
and daughter to the people of Maḣpiya Wakan. The buffalo
spirit helped both men and women alike, protecting hunters and
stimulating fecundity. It was generally believed that "young
buffalo cows may become like women" and that "their children
will be like the children of men," and also that "if they run
away, they become like cows, and their children become like
calves" (Walker, *Lakota Belief and Ritual* 124). But if a buffalo
can become human, then a human can be filled with the virtues
of the buffalo—courage, generosity, and the ability to further life.

In "Hokšila Wan" the buffalo woman's virtues remain in her
brother during her first, temporary absence: "Na wana koška-
laka k'un he oyate awanwicayanka" 'And now that same young
man watched over the nation' (Buechel, *Lakota Tales and Texts*
378). She is gone for one winter, a time of quiescence when
many forms of life are invisible. During this time the potentiality for new life is entrusted to the brother who now becomes
the embodiment of spiritual protection. The woman's return is

accurately forecast when the young man dreams of her setting out from a camp in the north where "šunkawakan ota unpi" 'they have many horses.' In effect, the implied strength of her people has been imparted to her well provisioned human relatives. But upon her immediate return she is "ataya watoglaya" 'unkempt' in her appearance, and the people fear her. It is as if they see supernatural power undisguised by the natural forms that usually soften its intensity. The woman becomes "herself" again in the act of quieting her infant nephew, and for a long time the daily life of the *hocoka* is without extraordinary events of any kind. Again, the narrator includes the uneventful as an event in a story that reflects a developing process rather than separate states of attainment.

And just as one may surely expect ordinary experiences, *wakan* manifestations periodically recur, as here when the woman supernaturally brings the people a herd of buffalo. Later, while the woman sleeps, her breathing frightens the people because it sounds like that of a buffalo, but their fear will open into recognition of continual metamorphosis and increasing wisdom. Because their traditions have prepared them for miracles, the people are eventually calmed rather than shocked to learn that their sister is a buffalo woman. She tells them to witness her departure the next morning as if to demonstrate that "legends" have an ever-present immediacy. The compassion of the white buffalo woman who brought the pipe is continually repeated by spirits who take human form to renew the people's confidence and love: "Misun, tiblo, ina, oyate kin niwanicapi kta tka heon oyate kin misun niwicayin kta ca heon lel wahi ye" 'Younger brother, older brother, mother, your nation will live and therefore younger brother will lead them and that is why I have come' (Buechel, *Lakota Tales and Texts* 379). Spirits also take sensory form in the audible words of a story.

As the story nears its end, the buffalo woman announces her permanent departure. As *pte san win* (a white buffalo woman) rolled and became *pte san wan* (a white buffalo), so the heroine of this story "icaptanptan kic'un na inajin" 'rolls and stands' before she assumes her other form. The visible transformation affirms a continual movement of guardian spirits between the worlds. Like a scout or a warrior bringing news to celebrate, the sister "charges" out her last encouragement: "na etanhan kato-naunk kigla na paha unhe ekta akanl kiyahan na glakinkinyan najin. Na mahel kigla" 'and then she galloped toward her home and stopped on top of that same hill and then she moved in a zig-zag line and stood again. Then she disappeared over the other side' (Buechel, *Lakota Tales and Texts* 380).

Her elation overshadows a few tears shed for separation, perhaps for mortality. But the tears are soon "henala" 'sufficient' as the story returns to its purpose of honoring the Lakota vision of the world and offering it to mature listeners to preserve for those who are young:

> Na wana lila wicaceya. Na wana henala. Na hakela k'un lila yuonihanpi na tawicu cinca ko. Ho le hetanhan hoksi ha-kakta kin oh'an wastepi nanakun wohitikapi.

> And then there was much crying. And then it was enough. And they honored Hakela greatly and also his son. And so from then on that youngest son's deeds were good and also brave' (Buechel, *Lakota Tales and Texts* 380).

Life goes on in a good way only when a voice is spoken close to where the *niya* breathes. Such narrative *pejuta* (medicine), just above the understanding of the young, will protect them until they can watch over the growth of the next generation.

EIGHT

Akicita of the Thunder

Black elk's dedication to perpetuating Lakota traditions (Holler, "Lakota Religion" 27–28; *The Sixth Grandfather*
334) corresponds to the emphasis on transmission in the preceding oral narratives. The transformation of each Hakela into a
potent carrier of Lakota consciousness is initiated by their helpers
in individualized *sicun* (the sword and the scalp lock medicine).

In *The Sixth Grandfather* the agent of development assumes its
dominant collective form in the horses of the Great Vision and
the horse dance. Although the different colored horses represent
the characteristics of the four directions, the horse as an animal
species is an *akicita* (messenger), or potential embodiment of the
tonwan (physically manifest power, see Walker, *Lakota Belief and
Ritual* 230) of only one direction—the Thunder beings of the
West. DeMallie points out that the Great Vision is a Thunder
being vision but that Neihardt minimized this to avoid duplicat-
ing the dog or *heyoka* vision (also brought by the Thunder beings), and to censor entirely the *iwizilya akicita* (soldier weed)
given to Black Elk by a black horse rider (Thunder being), who
becomes a gopher, which then becomes the herb itself. These
transformations imply that the scourging power of the weed
exists in many possible forms. It is not necessarily confined to a
single destructive agent such as a nuclear weapon (to which it is
compared by Castro 95).

Before a battle, war horses were made receptive to the Thunder power through symbols:

> The whole flank behind the one line and the shoulder and
> leg in front of the other line are covered with small circular

markings, giving a somewhat dappled effect. These marks represent either cloud forms or hailstones; in either case, they are closely associated with thunder power . . . as the thunder bird rides the storms in safety, as the eagle, the hawk, the raven—related to the spirit bird—in the swiftness of their flight and the strength of their endurance escape the rain of hailstones and rise above the ferocity of the whirl-wind, so may the bearer of these symbols go safely through battle. (Blish 65)

The lightning and hail marks are present in *Black Elk Speaks,* as is the association of the swallow with the thunder, although the butterfly, which plays an important part in the unedited version, is not presented as the thunder's *akicita* in Neihardt's version. Since the horses of the North, East, and South are also decorated with lightning streaks in the Great Vision and the horse dance, the connection between purification, enlighten-ment, and the power of destruction provides a significant con-tinuum. An explosive emergence of sound and light begins the Lakota cycle of maturation. The progressive stages in the de-velopment of wisdom form the sequence of expression in sev-eral major ceremonies. Sun dancers are thrown to the ground, pierced, and required to dance attached to the sacred center by thongs. This is called "the captivity" and "the torture," but it is inseparable from the sacred tree that is the source of joy and re-newal. Spiritual completion is accomplished by "the release" when the bonds break through the dancers' flesh shortly before they "return" to the people who have always been with them just outside of the circle. The thongs attach the dancers to a sacred center, so that upon release that same center will hold everyone in a hoop of generosity and mutual sacrifice. The rit-ual repeats a dynamic change of recognition and a simultaneous alteration of reality since some of the people will live in the company of spirits, where no spirits had formerly been, after each sun dance has been performed. When the ordeal ends, for-getfulness of one's true identity ends.

The tree, the thongs, the suffering and "war" are valued, even loved. The dancer's scars are never boasted, but they become a lasting mnemonic of how a transformed understanding is brought about through sacrifice. The same metaphor of spiritual liberation may still be seen at any summer powwow in the sneak-up dance. The sneak-up song repeats many times *heyuha manipi* (they have him walking) as if to affirm the ability of all captives to return to being vigorously at-home-in-existence, however spiritually confined they may have been in a materialistic world. Even in the benevolent *Hunka* ceremony the man who is to be adopted as *hunka* is pushed out of a *tipi* with the announcement—"we should kill this enemy, but if anyone will take him for *Hunka* we will not kill him" (Walker, *Lakota Belief* 226). Then the man who has initiated the ceremony helps him up and affirms his intention to establish the bond. Like a sun dancer or a vision-seeker, a Lakota warrior underwent voluntary exile to keep poisonous spirits like *Gnaśki* (Crazy Buffalo) far from the *hocoka* (sacred circle) of confidence and love in which the *oyate* (nation) lived. The testing they endured banished divisive fear. The prayer to the west, with which so many Lakota ceremonies begin, recognizes that the abode of fearfully potent spirits is the best place for healthy conception to occur.

Just as the sun dance can be as trying to behold as to perform, so the horses in the Great Vision and in the horse dance "looked beautiful but still they looked fearful" (*The Sixth Grandfather* 217). The terrible aspect of an animal so familiar to everyday Lakota life develops from the horse's sudden appearance on the plains as the *śunkawakan* (literally, sacred dog), and probably from the exhilaration of risk in the buffalo hunt and in war. The speed of a horse is inseparable from the flow of energy and emotion in a skilled rider. Together *akicita* (soldier) and *śunkawakan* (horse) became a *wakinyan* (thunder being). Returning from a successful raid, warriors painted their faces black, the color of the thunder spirits whom they kinetically resembled. Densmore transcribes a horse song which communicates this connection, "kola/mitaśunke/kinyan yan/inyanke lo" 'friend/my horse/ flies like a bird/as it runs' (Densmore 299). The simile "like a bird" may be mistranslated here. *Kinyan* means only "it flies," not that the horse flies "like a bird" in the specific sense of *zintkala*. The Lakota spirit of the thunder is also "something that flies," Wakinyan, and the term, "Thunder bird" in the case of the Lakota is somewhat misconceived.

Wakinyan represents the potency and potentiality of the warrior spirit. He begins a process that culminates in the manifestations of tree-splitting destruction and life-giving rain, just as atmospheric percussion becomes the thunder of a *cega* (drum), the hail of a *wagmuha* (rattle), the neighing of a *šunkawakan* (horse), and the words of a *walowan* (singer): "anpao/hinape/cinhan/ šunkakan wan/hotonwe" 'daybreak/appears/when/a horse/ neighs' (Densmore 300). The predominant Lakota metaphor of this struggle for realization is that of mounted combat. Densmore's transcription of the thunder or *heyoka* vision of Lone Man opens with the dreamer's report of hearing thunder from the west becoming "the sound of hoofs, and I saw nine riders coming toward me in a cloud, each man on a horse of a different color" (Densmore 159). Nine riders then come from each of the other directions and the men tell him, as Black Elk was also told, to kill an enemy and thereby become "a member of their company" so that he might "always call on them for help in time of need." Although these riders come from four directions, they are all Thunder beings.

Not every Thunder dreamer had the power to present a *šunkawakan wacipi*. In a horse dance, the dreamer exercises the advanced ability to allow the entrance of just enough fear to evoke courage and cooperation in participants and beholders. The most significant difference between the horse dance reported by Frank Fools Crow and that of Black Elk is that Fools Crow's horses are wild (for additional variations, see Blish 39, Laubin 360–62, and Wissler 97–98). Their dangerous disposition is transformed by a man whose name suggests a special affinity for horses,

A fire was built next to the corral, and Poor Thunder made a medicine by taking some red-hot ashes and mixing them with the smoke. The horses had never been ridden and at first were frightened and unruly, stomping and rearing. But when Poor Thunder took his medicine over to the corral and let the wind blow it through the rails and across the horses, they calmed down in moments and were no longer wild. (Mails, *Fools Crow* 79)

Then in the dance each rider covers his face with a black cloth he can see through. Black is the color of the western powers, and the beholders may now "see through" Wakinyan's terrible aspect to his creative operation. Poor Thunder begins the process. His is the power of initiating a progressive growth through the Lakota virtues which flower in *woksape* (wisdom). His horse is therefore black, the color of inception, "Poor Thunder went to the black horse and petted it. Then without the aid of a bridle, halter, rope, or anything else, he climbed on top of it" (Mails, *Fools Crow* 79). Poor Thunder's beginning manifests the first of the Lakota virtues, *woohitika* (courage), making it possible for the other riders to successively mount their horses. Once the sudden dramatic act of *woohitika* has brought the riders astride, they must manifest *wawacintanka* (fortitude) by not losing their nerve and allowing the horses or their own excitement to bolt.

But a spiritual ceremony does more than display the virtues of the participants. The purpose of the ceremony is to bestow awareness on the beholders through the power of the third virtue *wacantognaka* (generosity). Courage and fortitude prepare the way for the pivotal event, the visible arrival of the spirits. Singing, the articulate act of evocation must precede this visitation, "then the singing began, and the horses started dancing, really dancing. I was so excited I could hardly stand it" (Mails, *Fools Crow* 80). The spirits of the thunder now enter into the horses. Certain animals can contain specific spirits to become the *tonwan* or embodied power of these spirits (see chapter 6). The thunder makes itself known through many things that fly such as the swallow, the dragonfly, or the butterfly, but among the *ši-toblayanpi* (four legged-beings), Wakinyan clearly favors the horse:

It had been a sunny day, but huge black clouds formed in the sky. Thunder began to boom, and about ten yards ahead of us, lightning started to strike. Amazingly the horses did not bolt and run. Whinnying and snorting, making all of the strange sounds horses can make, they danced straight toward the lightning. As they did so, the lightning moved in a semicircle, and we followed it while it kept striking ahead of us in a broad flashing curtain of light. Not once did the wild horses run away or even turn their backs. (Mails, *Fools Crow* 80)

The horse dance welcomes difficulty to dispel fear in ritual motion: "Poor Thunder and I started to sing and pray, and the storm and the lightning split in two, as though the curtain of light were torn in half from top to bottom. The power of our prayer did this" (Mails, *Fools Crow* 80). The prayers are potent because the riders have accepted thunder in the heavens and in the wildness of the horses with courage and respect. They hold no illusions of favored safety, however. After the ceremony the horses are *watogla* (wild) once again and "they took off running as fast as they could go" (Mails, *Fools Crow* 80). Fools Crow emphasizes the unpredictability of existence in general, represented by the wild horses and the Thunder beings they temporarily contained, "there was a great amount of thunder and lightning, and it was a terrifying time. The performance of the horses was truly amazing" (Mails, *Fools Crow* 80). The terror makes the miracle possible. Terror is the seed spread by the Thunder beings and it grows incrementally into *woohitika* (courage), *wawacintanka* (fortitude), *wacantognaka* (generosity), and *woksape* (wisdom).

This dynamic process is not understood as an achieved advancement from point to point, but as the gradual acceptance of the whole process, and the ability to observe its states of development synchronistically without interpersonal or temporal divisions. Such fullness of perception is usually preceded by a sacrificial emptiness—fasting in the ceremonies—poverty in the oral narratives. At the beginning of "The Gift of the Horse," the fifty-third story of Ella Deloria's *Dakota Texts,* poverty has prepared a man to receive power to strengthen his people, who reveal themselves to be spiritually poor by their selfishness. Although they have an abundance of meat and other necessities because they have camped all winter near "plenty of buffalo," they do not provide even one strong horse to a poor man and his wife to allow them to come along. The couple subsists for a time on scraps of bone and meat strewn around the abandoned campsite until one day the man ascends a hill, as men do when they seek a vision, though he is only seeking rest from gathering wood. Nevertheless, he suddenly perceives the physical form through which the spirits will reward his virtue and his will to live. A black-spotted stallion comes over the eastern horizon to take a drink in a lake, after which it lies down, rolls, and goes back toward the east until it disappears (cf. the buffalo woman, chapter 9). Although the horse arrives from the east, its black markings identify its *tonwan* as that of the west, and its spots represent the hail. Its coming to drink foregrounds water (Black Elk's curative cup is analogous) as another identifying sign.

A little grey bird immediately arrives to give the man a special medicine which, like that of Poor Thunder in Fools Crow's horse dance will have power to convert a wild horse, or an immature understanding, into a being whose full energies are concentrated into serving the people. To accomplish this, the man must impart his own spiritual power to a mediating symbol, as Black Elk does when his Great Vision is enacted in the horse dance. In the oral narrative the horse's head is first caught in a rope as the people's attention is caught in the hoop of a ceremony. Then the man chews a medicine root brought to him by the spiritual messenger, the grey bird, and after rubbing some on himself, he blows the rest on the horse's nose, so that the horse stands still and quietly lets the rope be put around his neck. A willingness to serve the people is realized through the usual sequence of transmission—a spirit sends a messenger (the grey bird) to a man who, through a symbolic medium, changes the life of the beholder (the horse). The effect of the medicine as a spiritual medium also strengthens the mare the man already owns and makes her fertile.

From a humble receptiveness to mystery, and from a will to unstinting generosity, three miraculously swift colts are born that are a source of delight and confidence to the whole tribe. But the invigoration of mysterious favor can be dissolved by

simple jealousy. When someone tries to cut the picket line outside the man's lodge, the horse articulately alerts the man to the
thief's intention to "teunyanpikta" 'cause our death.' The disap-
pearance of a *wakanyan* (sacredly lived) harmony is always imminent. The man emerges to return the people to a sense of self
protectiveness:

> Śunka wakan ki lena aimayaħaħapikta ca wicabluhaśni ye-
> lo. Niyeś oyate ki iniwaśtepikta un lena wicabluha caś wa-
> yakuwapi ca nicinca wotapi k'un; na nakunś ozuye c'an
> wicanunpi na un wicoħan waśteśte slolyayapi k'un. Śun-
> kawakan ki lena wowacinyepi ca nazinpe lo.

> I do not keep these horses in order that you shall insult me
> through them. I keep them for the sole purpose of bringing
> good to the tribe, and in that spirit, I lend them to you to
> hunt meat for your children, as you know; you have also
> used them freely in war and, as a result, have achieved
> glory. These horses stand here to serve. (E. Deloria, *Da-
> kota Texts* 258–59)

Supernatural power must be used only to defend and nourish
the nation. If any individual tries to selfishly exploit a blessing
conferred on the whole people, such as the sacred pipe, then all
the people suffer. The influence of such anti-generative greed is
noxiously contagious. The people need to breathe in an atmo-
sphere of healthy symbolic expression or they will be "watogla"
'wild' and "itanyeśni" 'useless'. The thunder horse recalls the
consequences of forgetting gratitude and generosity:

> oyate ki le el taku iyuha ogna tanyan yaunpikta ca micinca op
> migluota na un iniwaśtepi k'un, wicoħ 'an śica wan el hiyu
> ca wama hehayelakte lo. Ca ake śicaya yaunpikta tka he tuwa
> t'eunye-wacinpi ki he e ca oyate wawicakiyuśice lo.

> In order that you in this tribe might be fortunate in all
> things, I and my young have multiplied; and from that,
> you have benefited in the past; yet now, because an evil
> thing has entered the tribe, this source of good shall stop.
> You must go back to your former state when things were

hard for you, all because the one who tried to kill us has by his act brought it upon the entire tribe. (E. Deloria, *Dakota Texts* 259)

This power of preparing the soul for strenuous survival must be alertly maintained. The horses had been "ozuye c'an wica-nunpi na un wicoĥ 'an wašteŝte slolyapi" 'used freely in war and to win glory.' They must necessarily precede in fundamental value even the swift buffalo-runners used in the hunt. Only a secure and disciplined people can be receptive to a wisdom that stresses its own fragility. A ceremony or a story uses the power of the lightning to illumine the consciousness and to burn away superfluous needs. Only the fundamental details of living in a sacred manner are visible from the story's point of view, which is like the hill from which the man sees "wi hinape ci ogna taku hinapin" 'something coming over the horizon' after a long period of deprivation.

Among the *Wakan Tanka,* the initiation of life in a pure space was the task of Wakinyan, the flying one who lives in the west. He creates many forms of life, which he strengthens in the rigors of atmospheric and emotional storms. These storms are always in process at various stages of an individual's life, or on different places on the earth among varying forms of life. Wakinyan's appearance is terrible to behold because it communicates the insecurity of any natural state. His image in Walker's account suggests an innate part of being which always remains beyond consciousness:

He [Inyan, the Rock] made a shapeless creature and named him *Wakinyan* (Winged one or Thunderstorm). *Wakinyan* is as shapeless as a cloud and terrifying to behold. He has two wings of many joints, which he can spread afar or make very small; he has neither legs nor feet, but has huge talons that can pierce the hardest of things; he has no mouth, but has a huge beak armed with sharp teeth that can rend and tear the toughest of things; he has no throat, but has one voice that is the thunder; and he has no head, but has one eye, and the glance of that eye is the lightning. (*Lakota Myth* 213)

Wakinyan maintains a hidden dimension even when he is represented. The idea of his partial invisibility is important to his role as the initiator of wisdom and generation. Śkan, the *Nagi Tanka* (Great Spirit) and Sky-God, foresaw the necessity of this disguise, when he told Wakinyan, "hide yourself from all save only those evil ones whom you would destroy" (Walker, *Lakota Myth* 213). Śkan then teaches Wakinyan to make the clouds, "robes that are shapeless like himself" (Walker *Lakota Myth* 213). His true creative nature is further hidden by his consistently "unnatural" behavior: "when he is pleased he seems angry, and when he is furious he seems pleasant. He delights in opposition and contrariness" (Walker, *Lakota Myth* 214). This is a way of demonstrating that full development is reached only by remaining receptive to "negative" experiences. Wakinyan brings forth his young on the top of a high mountain where his lodge has no roof and where he rests on jagged rocks. From this foundation of intensely felt being Wakinyan flies forth to repel the enemies of growth—greed, pride, and the other invasive *wakan śica* (bad spirits) often personified in the oral narratives. The acceptance of Wakinyan's warrior aspect is essential to understanding the Lakota concept of creation.

Neihardt's omission of the soldier weed, the warrior power of Black Elk's vision, and even Black Elk's reluctance to acknowledge its potential benefit, should not deter us from remembering that Wakinyan's war power must cleanse the world before he can release potential life into pulsing motion. In Walker's cycle of Lakota mythology the Thunder's rage against pollution precedes his ability to create. Wakinyan initiates plant life on the earth after he has purified its surface. Other powers then further the life cycle but Wakinyan creates the *itkasupi* (seeds, eggs, cocoons, and wombs of various kinds). He also makes possible the duration of life in transformed states when he obtains water by a swift raid over the seas from which he steals rain to make spiritual fruition possible. Wakinyan is necessary for reproduction and his powers are most potent at the stage of inception. As in ceremonial communication, Wakinyan moves each plant and each person to contain seeds.

Although Wakinyan hatches his young in a great nest, his primary role, especially in terms of traditional Lakota society, is male. He protects the people by roaming the world. As he travels, evils become familiar. He knows his targets and how to strike them, and when he passes over or through the people, he knows how to speak to them. The spirit of Wakinyan may be heard in the hoofbeats of his *akicita,* the horse, and he is brought into a ceremony in the hail of the rattles and the thunder of the drums. These sounds attract benevolent spirits to assist the people and by entering a circle where these sounds are made, the spirits show their respect for Wakinyan. Since Wakinyan impels the process, the other spirits and the people respond by helping to complete it. The *Cega Tanka Oyate* (Thunder being Nation), which arrives to cheer on the horse dance, rejoices because the people have received the Thunder's incipient words and celebrate their embodiment.

Wissler reports how an equine *akicita* of Wakinyan inspired various incarnations through the Oglala Horse Society, which possessed medicines to capture wild horses, to make war horses faster, to heal their wounds, and to cure their ills: "A man went up on a high hill to fast. After four days a figure appeared to him. As it approached, it was seen to be a person. This person explained the rules and formulae. Then he became a horse and disappeared among the thunders" (Wissler 96). Soon after a man captures a black striped buckskin stallion. Black is the color of potentiality, yellow is the color of growth. The leader of the horse dreamers immediately sees what the horse is and orders it to be released: "At once, there was a great cloud; the horse went into it. Then it rained and thundered, the lightning flashing between the tipis. In the center of the storm, they saw the horse rising to heaven, his halter still trailing behind" (Wissler 96). Respect for the thunder horse progresses inevitably to the regeneration of life. Four remarkably swift horses are soon captured. As in Deloria's oral narrative they breed descendants from which a *wakan* power flows to the people.

Many stories are told of the mystical rapport between men and horses. Bushotter reports several incidents of wounded men being rescued by their horses in the heat of battle. As in the case of other spiritual powers, the appropriate symbolic expression could transform a horse from an ordinary animal to a sentient and sympathetic *wawokiya* (helper): "Some men consider that the horse is mysterious; and they have horse-songs. And it is said that when those songs are sung, the horses hear them and come to the place of the song" (E. Deloria, *Teton Myths* 56:1). The sound symbols of a song can evoke friendship from these spirited animals; the visual symbols, especially of the thunder as reported by Blish, encourage the horses to "act properly" in battle: "they include them with the warriors as fighters, and tie rattles or small bells around their necks" (E. Deloria, *Teton Myths* 56:1). But the most dramatic sensory interplay between a spirit's *ton* (direct manifestation) and *tonwan* (embodied manifestation, see Walker *Lakota Belief and Ritual* 230) occurred in the rite of *śunkawakan wacipi* (the horse dance).

The horse dance fully unfolds the seed implanted in Black Elk at the age of nine. The Great Vision begins with a visitation from Wakinyan and continues with instruction by him in the various forms which allow him to "quickly pass from one place to another so that he may appear to be many when he is but one" (Walker, *Lakota Myth* 214). A vision is intended to foretell, in the sense that a seed foretells, what Black Elk will do for his people or more generally how a human being can redemptively transmit courage and vitality to his *takuyepi* (relatives). The related word *wakinya* (not Wakinyan) means "to foretell accurately" and "to initiate, to begin." Neihardt missed the initiatory role of the thunder, as DeMallie explains:

> In the notes the men tell Black Elk "Your Grandfather is calling you," referring to the first (western) grandfather; *Black Elk Speaks* has "Your Grandfathers are calling you!" generalizing to all six grandfathers. The cloud house where the grandfathers sit in council is in the west, and it symbolizes the home of the western grandfather. Throughout the stenographic notes, Black Elk varies between referring to the grandfather(s) in the singular and in the plural. It seems that he understood himself to have been called by the west-

ern grandfather (for it was to that direction that he went) but that the Western grandfather represented all six grandfathers. (*The Sixth Grandfather* 94)

Just as all the spirits are embraced by *Wakan Tanka* (the great mystery) so in Black Elk's vision all the spirits are phases of the spiritual maturation that begins with the Thunder power. De-Mallie stresses that the predominance of the Thunder in the stenographic record was not translated into *Black Elk Speaks* with its reduced emphasis on "thunder and lightning, horses, dogs, swallows, butterflies, dragonflies" each of which functions as a specific representation of the western powers (*The Sixth Grandfather* 99). When Black Elk enters into the first instructive form, the "cloud-tipi," Neihardt does not tell us, as Demallie does, just which power is exclusively associated with this kind of lodge. Walker reports the tradition of clouds being the garments of Wakinyan. Similarly, a Lakota rainbow is symbolic of the Thunder beings. The rainbow represents the mediating presence of visible form extending invisible sources of power. Black Elk named Neihardt "Flaming Rainbow," "because wherever his words fall, they make the earth greener. And when his words have passed, the memory of them will stand long in the west like a flaming rainbow" (Whitney 20–21). The rainbow is an especially good symbol of mysterious revelation; the form which mediates between the visible and invisible worlds. Elk dreamers called their hoops "rainbows," because "part of the rainbow is visible in the clouds, and part disappears in the ground. What we see is in the shape of a hoop" (Densmore 259).

NINE

Tatanka Iyacin:
To Be Like the Buffalo

To THE EXTENT that it appears at the end of a cycle, and from its obvious visual properties, a rainbow represents wholeness or at least wholeness within the development of one who has been favored by the Thunders. But Lakota society in the largest sense required the balance and infusion of powers supplied by many spirits through many dreamers. As strongly and even more inclusively than the Thunder power, the buffalo offered ceremonial metaphors of identity to the Lakota, just as its body became theirs in food, clothing, and most of the objects from which they derived the strength to survive.

In order to understand the context of Black Elk's expression as a Lakota whose male identity was formed in the old culture, something of the vast range of buffalo imagery should be suggested. The third Grandfather of the east shows Black Elk a man painted red who changes into a buffalo, which in turn charges toward the eastern horses, turning them into more buffalo (*The Sixth Grandfather* 118). Later the same man turns into a buffalo again, rolls on the ground and becomes a healing herb: "After the buffalo's arrival the people looked better and then when the buffalo turned into an herb, the people all got up and seemed to be well" (*The Sixth Grandfather* 128–29). Prevalent meanings of the color red and of the buffalo as the generous agent of nourishment and health are more fully expressed in Walker's account of the sun dance than directly by Black Elk. Nevertheless the more generalized buffalo spirit represents Black

Elk's societal role and that of all Lakota men and women, while the Thunder powers are specialized gifts for individual contribution.

As is appropriate for a Thunder being vision, Black Elk's metaphors express the cycle of spiritual growth as beginning with the thunder and ending with the rainbow. Aspects of the experience are embodied in swallows, butterflies, dragonflies, dogs, and especially horses. Although the animals and powers of the other directions are included, western metaphors predominate. The sun, the eagle, and the buffalo, on the other hand, express the powers of the east and predominate in the sun dance, *hunka,* and buffalo woman ceremonies. If thunder, lightning, and horses express sudden inspiration and courage in a young person, the sun and its *akicita* (messengers) represent mature fecundity, nurturing, and protection. The sun dance traditionally occurs at the summer solstice when plant life is in full flower and when the buffalo are gathered into large herds, embodying a "people" equipped with a way of being that guarantees vigorous survival. Undoubtedly this perception was influenced by the animals' ability to live though severe winters without shelter, but even more by their instinct to protect other members of their herd from attacks by predators. Even today visitors to state and national parks will notice that bulls wait to see if all members of the herd have crossed a road before they move on.

This is the ideal behavior of the mature warrior and vision seeker, and the purpose of the strength he has gained. A vision seeker like Black Elk leaves his mother and father but is not meant to love the Grandfathers more than his human parents. Spiritual power exists to protect the people. Christians are educated in their religion so that their souls may reach heaven, perhaps to join their relatives there. All strenuous work in Lakota society is directed toward relatives here. Early missionaries were hard pressed to convert members of a culture for whom cooperation between relatives was the primary value to a preference for subjection to a sovereign: "For I am come to set a man at variance against his father, and the daughter against her mother, and daughter-in-law against her mother-in-law . . . He that loveth father or mother more than me is not worthy of me: and he that loveth son or daughter more than me is not worthy of me" (Matthew 10:35,37).

Sacrifice was not undertaken to be "worthy" of protection by a savior but rather "tatanka iyacin" 'to be like the buffalo.' In Thunder metaphors, the Lakota could not "love" the thunder as the source of the process more than its culmination in the rainbow. In the eastern power metaphor, the source of the process is the sun, its culminating embodiments are the buffalo and the people, renewed as relatives through the sun dance. The potentiality, development, and fulfillment of essential human qualities are represented by the buffalo. Even the square of ground, cleared for the sun dance altar in the tipi of each man who pledges to dance, has curved lines extending from each corner as its "horns" to guard against malevolent beings (Walker, *Sun Dance* 69). The warrior power that begins with thunder in a predominantly western vision here begins with buffalo horns as the will to protect the traditional metaphors in which the people live.

A buffalo skull with a red stripe across the forehead to match a similar stripe on the pledger's forehead begins the extensive process of making man and buffalo relatives. Two additional stripes down the side of the skull "indicate that the buffalo god has adopted the candidate as a *hunka,* or relative by ceremony. The red stripes on the sides of the skull indicate that the Buffalo god will give especial protection to the candidate" (Walker, *Sun Dance* 69). In this initial phase, carried out by only two men, the pledger and a former sun dancer, the process of transmission from spirit to man is acted out. The two men smoke a pipe ceremonially to connect themselves with the strength to sacrifice for the people so obviously evident in the buffalo. Both the buffalo and the Lakota display the presence of the buffalo spirit in all their expressions; here their visible breath blows "the smoke into the nostril cavities of the skull, thus smoking in communion with the Buffalo god" (Walker, *Sun Dance* 70).

As in Black Elk's Great Vision, the color red connects the sun and the buffalo, the buffalo and the men, and the men to each other. Red is the penultimate color in Black Elk's directional circuit (other medicine men have different color sequences), and therefore Black Elk's buffalo man carries the herb that precedes the four-colored daybreak star herb. The sun dance performed in midsummer represents the full strength of mature individuals exercising the red "vitality" that produces new yellow life, the color of buffalo calves and the culminating south. As a celebration of tribal continuity the sun dance is the only Lakota ceremony in which a whole band or several combined bands of people gather in a large group. Various aspects of the ceremony emphasize the harmonizing of relationships in society, so that the unusually large assembly has a symbolic aspect in itself. Walker's explanation of the buffalo's role as "patron of sexual relations, generosity, industry, fecundity, and ceremonies" (*Sun Dance* 84) is consistent with the initiation of young men into the trying reality of being the ones upon whom survival depends.

For this inner transition to occur, ceremonial practice instills the buffalo qualities into the young men through an imaginatively resourceful creation of metaphors. In a large council *tipi* the individual pledgers, their mentors, the sun dance intercessor, and women for whom the buffalo ceremony (still to be described) has been performed, assemble to partake further of buffalo power before the severe ordeal begins. Just outside the *tipi* a buffalo head with red stripes painted on it is set down facing the sun. A fire kindled from buffalo chips burns beside it, in front of which the holy man sits. Then the mentors, buffalo women, and the people form concentric circles around the center, which radiates generosity, courage, and the other buffalo virtues into them. This diffusion of buffalo virtues and their translation into symbols with the power to make grow is again represented by the smoke of the pipe, lit from the fire of buffalo chips and blown into the nostrils of the buffalo head (Walker, *Sun Dance* 98).

As the buffalo spirit makes its living presence visible in this conventional metaphor of smoke, so other senses receive the message of protective abilities granted by the spirits and alive in the people. Sweetgrass represents the ability to communicate with benevolent spirits and to introject their qualities. The holy man burns some in the smoke to indicate the means of attracting all good influence, here specifically concentrated on the buffalo spirit. Next the buffalo women offer ornaments that the holy man attaches to the horns to show the esteem held by the people for the buffalo spirit (Walker, *Sun Dance* 98). If people do not value the survival qualities granted by empathizing with the spirit, then unlike the buffalo animal, they will surely die.

In the feast that follows, the families of the pledgers provide buffalo tongues, considered the most desirable part of its body to everyone present. It is the last food to be consumed by the pledgers before they fast and helps to supply the requisite generosity and courage (Walker, *Sun Dance* 98). Like a vision seeker or a warrior who has acquired power from the spirits in a vision, the buffalo has been favored by the sun so that he can direct a power greater than his own to his relatives (Walker, *Lakota Myth* 299). On the first day of a four-day ceremonial cycle before the four days of the dance itself, the people form a procession to honor the buffalo spirit. In four circuits of the camp circle, families as well as young unmarried women praise the spirit of sexuality and harmonious domestic relations: "At dusk the young men sound the flute and young women go to trysting places, while the old men shake their rattles and the old women make incense of the bark or twigs of cottonwood" (Walker, *Sun Dance* 104).

As sacred drama the sun dance acts out the integration of sexuality into the healthy balance of human experience that characterizes Lakota cultural values. The young people participating in and observing the dance are learning a way of fulfilling their individual desires without creating conflicts among their relatives. Every human characteristic exists beneficially in balanced relation to the others. Evil or sickness results from disproportion, as personified in the giant, Iya, or the oddly shaped trickster, Iktomi. Health requires the inclusion even of potential weakness. Yumni, the childish spirit of the whirlwind is one of the sixteen aspects of the Great Mystery in the sense that infantile qualities remain beneficially present in adults (Walker, *Lakota Myth* 304–7). Transformation and wholeness rather than moral choice characterize Lakota psychology in many ceremonies.

The sun dance tree is captured like an enemy after which it is ritually transformed into the ceremony's central source of power. In part of this transformation sexuality is portrayed as both dangerous to the group's survival and the means of its creative perpetuation. The rawhide cutouts of Iya and Gnaśki, each with exaggeratedly long erections, portray enemies ruled by soul-constricting drives, much like the bad scout in the pipe-woman story (*The Sixth Grandfather* 283–85). By placing these images in the top of the tree, the people are admitting their prominence and preparing for the sacred drama of defeating them. This defeat is strategically accomplished by their prior admittance (see Chapter 6). Iya, the lurching monster of stupid appetite and Gnaśki, a malevolent fomenter of hatred and rage represent prime causes of internal violence and vulnerability to outside attack (see Walker, *Lakota Myth* 217). They are placed next to the bundle of sacred objects that contains the "potency of the Buffalo god," the force of love, cooperation, and personal sacrifice (Walker, *Lakota Belief and Ritual* 67). The images are formally tied to the pole before it is erected by a *heyoka* as if to say that they are to be carefully noted, like the *heyoka's* behavior, so that the people may remember the value of negative example. (see Chapter 5)

All the men involved in setting up the pole, from the hole digger to the men who place it upright, to the men who put the dirt back in the hole, work with hands painted red to represent the turning of ordinary hands or people into those capable of living in a sacred manner (Walker, *Sun Dance* 97). Buffalo fat is placed in the hole to impart its essence to the pole and finally to the sun dancers who are attached to it by the rawhide ropes and who embrace it to pray (Densmore 118). Their sacrifice requires courage, which cannot exist without love for the people. Ordinary men would not suffer for others and would employ their potentialities only to gratify themselves. A healthy nation must be composed of extraordinary individuals, and therefore natural (selfish) adolescent sexuality must be recognized as an enemy until an equally natural and purposeful sexuality can take its place. Pauline-Augustinian Christianity considers sexuality to be evil, but in the old sun dance it was recognized as a spiritual force benevolently channeled by ritual (c.f. modern sun dances which omit sexual symbolism; Amiotte, "Lakota Sun Dance" 63; Mails, *Fools Crow* 124, and *Sun Dancing* 121).

Instead of tearing Iya and Gnaśki down immediately, a feat significantly difficult because of their height at the top of the pole, the people have a more ingenious and devious way of dealing with such an eminent obsession. As in a healing ceremony where the patient initially personifies fear, the men and women enact their sexuality to return from destructive magnification:

> Then the people may shout the names of Iya and Gnaśki and protest that these Gods prevail in the camp. Immediately, men and women commingle and then follows a period of license when they banter each other and jest of sexual things. At that time a man or a woman may be familiar with one of the opposite sex in a manner that would be an indignity at other times, and the ribald merriment may become boisterous. (Walker, *Sun Dance* 110)

But before the enemy can indeed prevail, warriors dance a war dance, i.e. they use a countering symbolic expression to gather and concentrate the strength that was in danger of diffusion. They then shoot arrows at the cutouts until they fall, after which buffalo selflessness is once again made to replace disproportionate appetite (Iya) or ruthless egotism (Crazy Buffalo): "The Superior should quickly make an incense of buffalo chips on the altar, to appease the elevated fetish and when the chips have burned to coals he should scorch the fallen images on these coals and thereby destroy their potency for evil" (Walker, *Sun Dance* 110).

When the people have finished cheering, the intercessor further reveals the sexual "theme" of the sun dance by leaning a dried buffalo penis against the pole and next to the most sacred object, the pipe. Sexuality has become a metonymy of healthy growth, especially appropriate for the (usually) young participants in the dance. The one who lives only for himself will not progress, just as Iya and Gnaśki have been shot down. To undergo a full cycle of human growth, to reach the solstice, the potencies of a human being must be used as the buffalo penis is used, to recreate the full scope of awareness and behavior possible for a species. With a consistent ability to channel the sources of power into full growth, represented by Black Elk in the rainbow or the four-rayed herb, an ordinary person in a limited, instinctively moved physical body can receive the "cheers" of the Grandfathers (*The Sixth Grandfather* 138).

The crucial concentration on the center as source, process, and fulfillment, is expressed in the basic "choreography" of the sun dance proper, but even before that in Walker's account, candidates were tested and strengthened in their ability to keep the virtues of the buffalo as the central purpose of their acts. Immediately before the sun-gazing dance, the pledgers enact the Buffalo dance in which they move around the buffalo skull imitating the pawing of a buffalo bull, taking in the spirit of that powerful animal's preparation to fight as they approach their ordeal. While conflict and pain must be known, the ability to endure them depends on remembering the buffalo virtues at the center. The survival of warriors or visionaries in violent motion outside the camp circle depends on remembering one's family at the center. For young men this must become natural. At first one may be tempted to see only honors for oneself, to look outward at the enemy more than inward toward the circle, to forget everything but personal glory:

> While dancing they must gaze continually at the ornamented buffalo head. The red marshals should watch them, and if one of them ceases to gaze at this head they should admonish him; and if he persists in looking away from it they should conduct him to his robe. One thus removed from this dance loses the privilege of becoming a buffalo man. Those who dance the four periods of this dance become buffalo men. (Walker, *Sun Dance* 115).

In the sense that buffalo bulls put the safety of the herd before their own, the purpose of the sun dance, its attendant rites, and other ceremonies is to make people into buffalo in that they become animated by the buffalo spirit. After the men become buffalo in the buffalo dance, they demonstrate their new power by transmitting it to the people. First they are given a stick with a buffalo tail attached to it, and by this means they drum on a dried buffalo hide, singing their courage into the small children who are about to undergo the ear piercing ceremony. The parents too need the support of these songs, since they "should not heed the cries of the babe until its ears have been pierced and then the mother should take and comfort it" (Walker, *Sun Dance* 116).

The buffalo men should include those who are to be pierced or drag buffalo skulls in the current sun dance as well as those who have been buffalo men in the past. The buffalo dance and the sun dance turn adolescent boys into men, human beings into buffalo in the prevailing metaphor. While the willingness to defend the people is the buffalo trait emphasized in the sun dance, absolute loyalty is associated with the buffalo in the *hunka* or making of relatives ceremony. The one who conducts the ceremony wears a buffalo horn cap as is worn by some sun dance intercessors, and a buffalo skull on the altar in the *hunka tipi* is the ceremony's central symbol. Dishes separately containing lean meat and fat meat are placed on either side of the skull. Then the holy man thanks the skull for giving the meat and ritually returns a portion of it to the buffalo spirit (Walker, *Sun Dance* 127–28).

Then, burning sweetgrass over the fire, he again directly contrasts the spirit of the buffalo with that of Iktomi and Anog-Ite, mythological embodiments of egotism and seduction, asking the sun to keep them away from a circle where relatives are made, where loyalty reigns over personal satisfaction. Those given the special status of *hunka* manifest in a relationship of two what the relationship should be among all. Even before going to war where one must concentrate on the enemy and on physical survival, it must be recalled that the purpose of excursion is to prevent incursion. A warrior must make an offering to the "Buffalo, the patron God of nuptials and fecundity . . . of the chase and of providing" (Walker, *Sun Dance* 132).

Then in the middle of the ceremony, the bond of relationship is again expressed in its most common metaphor. A Lakota man lives to protect his own and to make growth possible. Offerings to the buffalo made by painting a rock red, the buffalo color, manifest these priorities and help to hold the buffalo and *hunka* spirit (also symbolized by a red stripe on the face) within a man:

> The Buffalo will cause your woman to be industrious and to bear many children. The Gods will protect you in war. They will keep your women and children from the enemy. If you listen to the Buffalo, He will aid you in the chase so that you will have plenty of meat and robes and so that the wolf will be afraid of you. (Walker, *Sun Dance* 134)

Blowing smoke through the nostrils of the buffalo skull has the same meaning as in the sun dance: "the Conductor . . . blew smoke . . . into the nostril cavities of the buffalo skull . . . and then gave the pipe to the young man, saying, 'smoke with the spirit of the buffalo, for you are now as its brother'" (Walker, *Sun Dance* 136). Man and buffalo have been given the power to protect their families, but if the man shows disrespect for his brother by neglecting to focus his mind on him, he will weaken and the people will die. As the *hunka* are pledged to help each other unconditionally, so the buffalo will feed, clothe, and inspire the people.

But if the buffalo bull was a model and brother to a young man, the buffalo cow was a symbol of fecundity and nurturance for a woman (see M. Powers 38, 67–70). In the girl's puberty or Buffalo ceremony, performed throughout the summer, the buffalo spirit sanctifies female sexuality in the same way that the sun dance ordeal sanctifies young men. The ceremony is prepared by the holy man wearing a buffalo horn hat as he again blows smoke through the nostils of the buffalo skull and paints a red stripe on its forehead (Walker, *Sun Dance* 145).

In this ceremony, unlike the others, the skull is that of the buffalo cow, but both male and female buffalo spirits are ritually addressed. The following song refers to the buffalo's call at rutting time: "Buffalo bull in the west lowing. / Buffalo bull in the west lowing. / Lowing he speaks" (Walker, *Sun Dance* 146). The "woman" to whom the bull buffalo calls initially "answers" through the holy man's words and ritual acts. The female buffalo spirit will become manifest in the ceremony and visible in the girl as she changes into a woman: "Bull buffalo I have painted your woman's forehead red and have given her a red robe. Her potency is in her horns. Command her to give her influence to this young woman so that she may be a true buffalo woman and bear many children" (Walker, *Sun Dance* 146). This is the fulfillment of the cycle of growth represented by the ceremony. The cycle begins with the girl's first menstruation. The discharge of menstrual fluid should be wrapped in a bundle and placed in a plum tree as an offering and emblem of the fruitfulness and hospitality favored by the buffalo spirit. The girl is taught the purpose of her sexuality and the necessity of placing it beyond the reach of "coyotes" or other beings of simple appetite.

Sexuality has a purpose, demonstrated to the girl and through the holy man by the buffalo spirit. Within the conventions of the sacred drama and the oral tradition, by which a negative example is foregrounded (Iktomi stories, or the cutouts atop the sun dance pole), the holy man presents a semi-comic, semi-frightening portrayal of Gnaśki (Crazy Buffalo) to prepare the girl for a similar approach by a young man. The holy man's portrayal helps to make such an approach far from flattering or seductive. After dancing to the girl and back to each direction with increasing speed, the "frantic" holy man gets on his hands and knees, paws the ground, and sniffs the air. When he crawls up to the girl, her mother puts sage under her arm and on her lap to repel the evil spirit (*Sun Dance* 148; cf. use of threat in healing, Chapter 6).

As if to show the efficacy of ritual gesture in purifying existence, the holy man immediately sits up and speaks: "That is the manner in which the Crazy Buffalo will approach you to tempt you to do things that will make you ashamed and will make your people ashamed of you. Your mother showed you in what manner you can drive away the evil things that would harm you" (Walker, *Sun Dance* 148). With the bull to defend her as well as her own ability to employ protective symbols like sage, the holy man begins to speak to her as if she has made the same transitions young men make in the sun dance. The mediating symbol is chokecherry juice rather than the pipe, and its color provides another link to the buffalo and the internalizing of the sun's vitality through its drinking: "We are buffalo on the plains and this is a water-hole. The water in it is red for it is sacred and made so by the Buffalo God and it is for buffalo women. Drink from it" (Walker, *Sun Dance* 148–49). As in other ceremonies the new identity passes into the spectators through the participants. Most Lakota ceremonies are performed for the onlookers as much as the participants, since all are passive in relation to the invisible spiritual current: "'My friends, this young woman gives you this red water so that you may drink of it and be her friends. Let all who are her friends drink of it.' He then passed the bowl and it was passed from one to another until all had sipped from it" (Walker, *Sun Dance* 149).

Vitalizing energy distributed from a concentrated receiver into the beholders characterizes the ceremonies discussed here, from Black Elk's horse dance, through the healing "dramas," to the sun dance. The girl's dress is removed and offered to one who needs it, after being spread over the buffalo skull. The receiver will also feel some of the power, focused in the girl by the sacred sage and sweetgrass she is given to eat, the food of the buffalo. Sources of strength can be internalized through careful attention to symbolic detail. After her mother arranges her hair so that the braids hang in front as a woman's do, the holy man paints the part red to relate her to the buffalo and to sanctify her sexuality. The "red" of her menstrual flow is no longer a simple bodily function but another reminder of the identity, vision, and purpose she shares. If she is conscientious about the external image, she will not be tricked by formidably distracting tricksters or monsters: "Red is a sacred color. Your first menstrual flow was red. Then you were sacred. You have taken of the red water this day. This is to show that you are akin to the Buffalo God and are His woman" (Walker, *Sun Dance* 149).

In the broader context of the buffalo symbols, Black Elk's description of a buffalo ceremony assumes an important place in his narrative, especially in light of the fact that Black Elk's predominant power was not associated with the buffalo. Still, Black Elk's vision was a comprehensive synthesis of Lakota symbols in which the red road and the buffalo have an immediate connection. The red road is walked by people who share the buffalo spirit:

> Then Red Dog made the sacred place like the buffalo wallow on the east side by the entrance. Red Dog also made the red road north and south across the circle and made buffalo tracks on either side of this red road, meaning that the people would walk buffalo-like and as a result would be tough. (*The Sixth Grandfather* 240)

And as endurance characterizes the buffalo and the sun dancers, so does the power to transfer their strength, initially accomplished by visual and verbal symbols: "I had buffalo horns on and was painted red all over my body and One Side followed painted red with a drum and a pipe filled with kinnikinnick" (*The Sixth Grandfather* 240).

Although the red buffalo in his vision gives Black Elk the right to participate, the ceremony is led by Red Dog (named Fox Belly in *Black Elk Speaks* 205), who derives the greater proportion of his power from the buffalo. Red Dog's song begins the manifestation of his power: "Revealing this they walk / A sacred herb, revealing it, they walk / . . . The sacred life of the buffalo, revealing it they walk / . . . Revealing a sacred eagle feather. Revealing it they walk. / The eagle and buffalo, relative-like they walk" (*The Sixth Grandfather* 241). The song effectuates the cure by tracing the movement of the spirit into the animal, from the animal to the singer, and from the singer to the people. While the eagle represents eternal endurance, the buffalo moves though the cycles of birth, death, and renewal.

In addition to healing the sick, the ceremony is a sacred drama vitalizing all beholders. As in the Buffalo ceremony transforming girls into women, the sick are moved to wholeness by a performance. The girl in the Buffalo ceremony learns to be repelled by Crazy Buffalo, while the observers of Black Elk's buffalo ceremony gradually come to resemble the buffalo spirit though repeated observation:

> After singing this song, Red Dog made a snorting sound of a buffalo and from his breath was visible red flames. I

could tell from this that he must have had a great vision about the buffalo, and he was a very sacred man . . . Then the sick made scarlet offerings in the same way, as they gathered around. The people were all eager to see me. In this act I represented the relationship between the people and the buffalo. (*The Sixth Grandfather* 241)

By imitating buffalo, the men are revealing the buffalo spirit, as in Red Dog's song.

In this and in other ceremonies, the holy man's purpose is to transmit the power to the witnesses until it is revealed in them as well. A person is often thought of as a garment or ornament selected to be "worn" by a spirit. The body, voice, and mind are felt to exist for the sole purpose of symbolically expressing that spirit: "The sun / is my friend / a hoop / it has made me wear / an eagle it has made me wear" (Densmore 139). The singer reveals the virtues he distributes but does not possess. The hoop and the dried eagle's body that he wears only emphasize the idea that his whole body is "worn" by the sun. Correspondingly, the cap, robes, armlets, and other buffalo parts worn in various ceremonies reveal that the wearers are worn by the sun, as do the eagle feathers and plumes of his other *akicita* (messengers). When a ceremony is completed, the spirit leaves the person. Its purpose is to benefit the people, and when it ceases to do this in symbolic expression, the person can rest. But if like Black Elk, just before the horse dance, the person is reluctant to become the spirit's persona, the person will suffer from excessive anxiety and nervousness. The spirit that comes to benefit the individual in a vision must be exhibited on a shield or a *tipi* cover, in a song, dance, or healing ceremony: "it was / a guard / predicted for me / a wind / wears me / behold it / sacred / it is" (Densmore 169).

The natural temperament of an animal helped to reveal the qualities of the spirit "wearing" it. Each Lakota person should be a buffalo person in the sense of being consistently generous, brave, hospitable, and willing to sacrifice for the people. But while some people are predominantly steady and strong, others like Black Elk and Crazy Horse have a special gift from the

Thunder beings of sudden and dramatic inspiration and expression. The horse is a skittish, more sensitive being than the buffalo. While any mature Lakota person must be steadier than a horse, i.e. part buffalo, some contribute sudden bursts of intense energy to the people's spiritual life. Crazy Horse was known for taunting the enemy by drawing their fire without being hit (Ambrose 134; Kadlecek 80, 89, 101, 117, 119, 128). Black Elk was similarly not wounded in battles after Wounded Knee, and his revival of Lakota spiritual life in 1931 was like a storm breaking a long drought.

All the powers were valuable and all had to balance each other. A whole nation of disciplined, loving people required replenishment in symbols to give vitality to ritual practice. The sun and the buffalo represent endurance, and the qualities needed to sustain it. Thunder horses bring impulses of new growth. The black of the west is the darkness from which life begins, manifesting itself as suddenly and inexplicably as thunder and lightning. The sweat lodge faces west (generally, although Black Elk has it facing east in *The Sacred Pipe* 32), because it effects spiritual rebirth, a new beginning in the darkness of its womb shaped space. The renewal is brought about by water becoming steam just as renewal in the plant world is caused by rain. But rain is infrequent during a northern plains summer. For daily social harmony the people must be like the sun and the buffalo, while in war and vision-seeking the thunders are usually invoked first.

Long term survival requires considerate predictability in men and women. Women live at the center, the symbol of generation in the sun dance, the point on which the male buffalo dancers and sun dancers must focus. Men who suspend or drag buffalo skulls attached to their backs circle the circumference for the women and children at the center. While the sun is male, it shines through the dancers to protect the female. Marla Powers points out that in ritual practice the buffalo was a "female" animal (69). In the *hunka* ceremony both male as well as female *hunka* acquired the qualities of the White Buffalo Calf Woman (Densmore 69), who brought the pipe so that the people would regard each other and the animal spirits as relatives.

At least three of the Lakota female virtues—chastity, fecundity, industry, and hospitality (M. Powers 67)—should also be foremost in the behavior of men when they are inside the circle. These virtues prevent the feuds and chaos which Iktomi and Gnaśki can occasionally foment. Sometimes the enemy must be vigorously driven away rather than steadily resisted. This activity can also endanger inner strength, and must be conducted at the spiritual and physical periphery. A man leaves the camp circle for war, hunting, or vision-seeking to bring it new life, and while he is outside, the male virtues of bravery and fortitude must take precedence. These same qualities would be destructive at home, if expressed with the intensity necessary outside the circle. Before and after a war expedition or vision quest, men were prepared in the sweat lodge to make the transition smoothly. Leaving a quiet, gentle state of being, they entered a world of pervasively felt danger from unknown spirits or human beings (see Black Elk's Dog vision, *The Sixth Grandfather* 227–31). The sudden reactions, mental and physical, enabling survival in this world would be grotesquely abusive directed toward women and children.

Since men were warriors and vision-seekers, the thunders and the qualities of the thunder were conceived of as exclusively male. Lakota men were more likely to be unpredictable or to have extraordinary experiences than were women, because they communicated regularly with dangerous animals, enemies, and supernatural spirits. The buffalo virtues remained at the "female" center of their being where they never forgot the women and children, but at the circumference men expected to suffer like sun dancers pulling away from the pole. For this reason a man had to acquire protective helpers in visions to accompany him in his travels. No matter what strange images moved before him, a man who held on to his pipe and trusted his helpers could not be hurt. And a warrior usually had a particular animal spirit, who had come to him in a vision, to protect him at crucial times in combat. Sometimes, as with Crazy Horse, the guardian can make the man "vanish like a ghost," or become "as the wind, and even in full daylight nobody can see him. Or

. . . he might be helped to take the form of a bird, and fly away," or the guardian spirit "may bewilder those who are inflicting suffering on him" (E. Deloria, *Teton Myths* 245:11–12).

Such a sudden infusion of strength was not part of most women's experience. Women were more like the buffalo all the time. "Pte" 'buffalo cow' is the generic term for buffalo (M. Powers 69). Men were subordinate to the female buffalo power in themselves within the circle. Outside the circle, however, in *hanbleceya* as well as in other activities a man's female (buffalo) self recedes. The sun dancer who drags buffalo skulls drags them *outside* the ceremonial circle but for the benefit of all within the larger camp circle. Sometimes protective activity requires the strength and steadiness exhibited in this form of the dance. At other times protectors actively take an equally necessary form, which must be expressed far from "home" in every sense.

The erratic movements of moths, butterflies, dragonflies, or swallows are embodiments of the spiritual experience of gifted men, who can instantly adapt to the irregularly emerging images of a vision, the swerving of a buffalo, or a charge by an enemy. On the other hand, women's experience was relatively constant, remaining at the center to nurture and provide conditions for growth. The *tipi* and all the material aspects of the camp circle, apart from weapons and personal clothing "belong" to the woman (M. Powers 82). But this is not to be equated with the Euro-American sense of possession. The camp circle is under the influence of the feminine spirit and when men are at home that spirit rules them there. A young man may be expected to be naturally egocentric, to be concerned with his own prestige and pleasure. Men and women in the *hunka* and Buffalo ceremonies are turned into buffalo. *Hunkayapi* concludes with both candidates tied together under a single buffalo robe. The ceremonies celebrate the feminine in all human beings. Little girls menstruate and become women who cherish wholesome life and protect it from coyotes. Young men act as *hunka* for all their relatives. They support and they nurture. The ceremony transforms male ambition through the ritual "capture" of one of the candidates at the beginning, to the female virtue of loyalty, exemplified by the White Buffalo Calf Woman, now reembodied in male and female holders of *hunka* rank.

The men joined as *hunka* treat each other with perfect generosity and wisdom, the two male virtues dominant at home. The four women's virtues—chastity, fecundity, industry, and hospitality—flow into connected acts, but the male virtues express a dual existence: courage and fortitude must be uppermost outside while generosity and wisdom rule a man at home. The virtues of *hunka* are not practiced toward an enemy. A man who becomes *hunka* makes himself fit to live in the woman's place. A man or a buffalo bull becomes more like a buffalo cow in times of peace, living comfortably at home with the herd. But when he faces predators on the outside he becomes the bull, and when he roams alone far from the herd, he is quintessentially male. To be masculine is to confidently let oneself be moved through sudden shifts of action and perception, to follow abrupt changes in the rhythm of all things, from riding a horse to a warrior dance. This becomes familiar to an experienced warrior. But a sun dancer is often just learning in his body to break free from the feminine sphere while keeping his eyes focused on it.

Small spherical stones were held sacred by the Lakota. Having been pushed up out of the ground by burrowing animals, they "lived" on different planes of existence (Powers, *Oglala Religion* 149). Such stones commonly carried by warriors and by modern Lakota people traveling off the reservation (W. Powers, *Sacred Language* 160) assure smooth transitions between the male and female spheres of being in the same way that sweat lodge ceremonies before and after *hanbleceya* (the vision quest) effect transition from the sacred world to one's relatives. A warrior or hunter rides to become part of a "dance" that does not ordinarily exist at home. Black Elk's horse dance focuses attention away from the center much more strongly than does the sun dance. A storm is attracted by the ceremony but does not fall on the camp circle. Warriors and vision seekers must endure storms so that the camp circle is safe.

Of all the spirits "remembered" by Lakota prayer the eagle alone is as important as the buffalo. Along with the buffalo's skull, hair, skin, and other parts, tail feathers and plumes from the eagle define another aspect of the Lakota to themselves. Women do not wear eagle feathers. The spotted eagle floating high in the sky is the protector of the people, like the warrior or vision seeker far from home (Powers identifies the spotted eagle as the immature bald eagle rather than the golden eagle, *Sacred Language* 148–49). The first sun dance song expresses wonder at the conversion of ordinary boys into conveyors of power: "Eca wanbli gleśka wan / u kta kehapi k'on / wanna u welo / wanna u welo" 'A spotted eagle you said was coming / he is coming now / he is coming now / now it comes' (Around Him and White Hat, Sr. 22).

In another sun dance song a prayer is sent "maka śitomniyan" 'all over the universe' so that the singer may continue to live with his relatives (Around Him and White Hat, Sr. 24). The spirit and body of the male Lakota had to follow the circuit of the song's voice, outward to the spirits first before life with the people could resume: "Tunkaśilaya, / hoye wayin kte, / namaȟ'on yeyo! / Maka śitomniyan / hoye wayin kte / namaȟ'on yeyo / mitakuye ob / wani kte lo / Epelo" 'Grandfather / I am sending a voice / hear me. / All over the universe / I am sending a voice / hear me / With my relatives I will live / That is all' (Around Him and White Hat, Sr. 24).

The work of a woman was also different from a man's. The making of clothing in particular required great patience and dedication. Sudden bursts of feeling or changes of thought could be distracting and cause mistakes that might take hours to undo if not immediately detected. A man, on the other hand, relied on just these reversals and irregularities to adapt to changed circumstances. While the sun dance turned men into buffalo bulls with an instinct to defend the helpless, it also made them eagles who must travel far to feed their young. Some visions, unlike Black Elk's, concentrated on certain phases of the life process represented predominantly by the buffalo and the eagle.

In the Great Vision and the horse dance, four virgins carry the most sacred symbol of each direction: the bow and cup of water, the white wing or herb, the pipe, and the flowering stick. Women bring life into the world but these women, like the White Buffalo Calf Pipe Woman and the girls who cut down the sun dance tree are virgins, not yet so mature in female powers as to displace the primarily male powers of the ceremony. The injunction against a menstruating woman being in proximity to a pipe or a ceremony prevents the neutralizing of male power by the excessive female emanation present at that time.

Neihardt has sick people bring "scarlet" offerings to all four virgins in the middle of the horse dance, though in *The Sixth Grandfather* only the virgin of the west receives the offering. The virgin who represents the black direction then offers the red tobacco ties to the west. Neihardt writes as if a cure were instantly achieved: "They all felt better and some were cured of sickness and began to dance for joy" (*Black Elk Speaks* 171). But Black Elk himself only says that the offerings were made to show that the spirits have "given me power to cure the people and to prove that I have really done this on earth" (*The Sixth Grandfather* 220). The virgin represents the turning of concentration from the female sphere to that of the healer. The healer is male and therefore receives his ability from outside the circle. The rest of the dance expresses the return of the vision hunter with spiritual food to be distributed among them all.

As in other ceremonies the movement of the dancers repeatedly advances to the quarters and returns to the center. At each directional point (omitted by Neihardt), the sick make red offerings to the virgin of the west who "represents all womanhood and the woman's part in the world and is there in behalf of the women" (*The Sixth Grandfather* 223). While most of the dancing motion is carried out by *akicita* (messengers) of the thunder, horses, and men, the virgins stand still to receive the benefit of kinetic prayer. Women again represent the permanent life of the Lakota people, while men represent the finding and supplying of all sources of strength.

An excess of feminine stability could immobilize beings that live primarily in motion. But motion without a center cannot transmit its energy into new life. In some modern sun dances male dancers are all counterbalanced by a single young woman who portrays the White Buffalo Calf Woman (personal attendance at 1983 Standing Rock sun dance). The virgins in Black Elk's Great Vision, unlike the horse dance are *all* dressed in red, the color of the buffalo. The western spirit tells Black Elk, "Behold your virgins all over the universe; through them the earth shall be happy. From all over the universe they are coming to see them" (*The Sixth Grandfather* 133). Then a song directs all energy toward the same female center: "My horses prancing they are coming from all over the universe" (*The Sixth Grandfather* 133). Black Elk remains both at and beyond the center throughout the dance, in that his bay horse is of the female earth but on its back is painted the solar spotted eagle, on which Black Elk sits. The grandfathers enable him to protect Lakota traditions by gaining an all encompassing perspective.

From the enduring constancy of the spotted eagle and through the culminating coalescence of the rainbow, Black Elk's vision impels creative motion on both the black and red roads. Outside the hoop on the black road of war, fasting, and isolation, a man acquires the strength to defend and, in the extraordinary case of Black Elk, recreate the hoop out of shattered fragments. As long as the people live, young men will have to walk the black road voluntarily even when the people and their culture appear to be content and safe. Without the return of those wearing black face paint (chapter 1), the people would sink into obsessive fear or oppressive security, but without the red serenity of ceremonies and domestic peace the center would not hold.

Employing the usual strategy of effecting a smooth transition to Christianity, missionaries changed the Lakota roads to Christian roads, as did Black Elk himself in *The Sacred Pipe* (chapter 1). Steltenkamp's 1987 interpretation is predictably non-Lakota: "all one can conclude from any of these passages is that traditional Lakota simply symbolized the virtuous life as being on a kind of 'good red road' and evil behavior as walking on a black one" (Steltenkamp 151). He goes on to an extreme Christianization of Black Elk's particular meaning: "Fervently wanting association with 'the good,' Black Elk implies the Christ event to be history's dividing mark. Hence, the red road, which on the map is identified with the Christian era, seems to be the path Black Elk prays his people might find and follow" (Steltenkamp 151–52). Nevertheless, Steltenkamp implicitly points up a difference between the Lakota roads and the Christian roads when he mentions that Black Elk's "Two Roads map," used in his missionary practice, has parallel non-bisecting roads, one a golden road to heaven, the other a black road to hell.

The difference could not be more succinct. The Christian roads represent a linear journey from birth to death, from Creation to Judgment Day, with differing destinations based upon moral choice. The Lakota roads are circumscribed within a circle of earthly existence, representing inevitable conflict and joy, regardless of moral action, sin and reward. In his Great Vision Black Elk is introduced to the black road as the place of the beings who have given him the vision and its powers to aid people in coming through disease, defeat, poverty and despair. The black road is revealed to Black Elk as a way of growth, not a byway to be avoided at peril to his soul: "Next the fourth grandfather pointed to the road from where the sun shines continually to where the sun goes down and said: 'Behold the black road, for it is the road of the Thunder beings' (road of fearfulness); or, 'Behold the black road for it shall be a fearful road. With this road you shall defend yourself'" (*The Sixth Grandfather* 118). Black Elk retrospectively adds an interpretation entirely at odds with the black road to hell cliché attributed to him by Steltenkamp: "Whenever I go to war I shall get powers from this fearful road and will be able to destroy any enemies. From the red road I get power to do good. From east to west I have power to destroy and from north to south power to do good" (*The Sixth Grandfather* 118).

Since the people have to leave the buffalo road in inevitable or ritualized adversity—sickness or *hanbleceya,* sorrow or the sun dance—they have acquired powers to aid them while they "fast." The Thunder power, in particular, had strengthened him. When rain is brought on a clear day by his concluding prayer, its extraordinary answer is missed by Neihardt: "a *scant chill* rain began to fall and there was *low, muttering* thunder" (my emphasis, *Black Elk Speaks* 274). These adjectives of failure obscure the confirmation of Black Elk's continuing kinship with the Thunder beings, and their corroboration of the several *hanbloglaka* (vision talks) Neihardt himself received. The narrative's conclusion predicts, as if it were crafted, the present state of Lakota culture, in which the red road is once again long enough for the people to walk.

CONCLUSION

The Metaphor Is the Message

In 1944 Black Elk told Neihardt the story of Sharp Nose, the Arapahoe, who recovered many stolen horses from the Crow by telling them falsely that he had been ordered to bring them a sacred bundle. When the Crow chiefs come to visit later, the Arapahoe chiefs confirm the "lie" so that a lasting peace is made among the tribes (*The Sixth Grandfather* 371–76). Sharp Nose took it upon himself to call an ordinary bundle sacred in order to help his people live. Black Elk's choice of this story may suggest much about his conception of truth. An inspired fiction occurs to Sharp Nose. His tribe had suffered the loss of their horses, as the Lakota had lost their land. Black Elk brings the whites a "bundle" in which he has wrapped the sacred symbols of Lakota religion. Perhaps he hopes to move them to return what they had taken from his people, despite an opposition as seemingly entrenched as that between the Crow and Arapahoe. If the vision or other parts of his life story are partly fiction, the grandfathers have approved Black Elk's resourcefulness and have given his metaphors the power to heal. Although Black Elk's verbal message may not have been sent in a verifiable bundle, the story operates to transfer opaque clichés into a rainbow, one that would help enemies to recognize themselves as relatives.

Black Elk's autobiography unfolds symbolically like sophisticated fiction. He intuitively selects details that add up to a coherent narrative (see Rice, *Lakota Storytelling* 40). The historical veracity of each detail cannot be established, nor can the consciousness of each visionary image be sorted out—sleeping dream, waking dream, real memory, imagined memory, imagined fiction, deliberate lie. In the horse dance, a man pretends to be a Thunder being; in the *heyoka* ceremony a man pretends to be a fool. The pretense is admitted, as in serious drama, but the effect is real in its creation of invisible qualities, physically represented in participants and beholders.

When Frank Fools Crow claims to heat the stones in his sweat lodge without fire, he may well be doubted (Mails, *Fools Crow* 97), but if he claims the power to transform and purify the lives of those who believe in him, the proof is immediately apparent. Lakota medicine men may speak metaphorically more often than is realized. Holler has pointed out that when a medicine man says, "the spirits told me you were coming," he is speaking conventionally rather than referring to ESP ("Lakota Religion" 22–23). The phrase is a greeting welcoming a visitor into a relationship that will be good, sanctioned by the spirits. When Fools Crow tells of how the spirits took him through the solid rock "door" of Bear Butte, he may be speaking of a dream (Mails, *Fools Crow* 182–83). And just as one would not expect a writer to explain that his fictions are not "real," so the truth of a vision is not determined on the basis of its occurring in a state of sleeping or waking. If a vision-seeker on *hanbleceya* falls asleep and dreams, that dream may be considered to be a vision (*The Sacred Pipe* 59). That Black Elk's Great Vision is a dream may be suggested by his description of himself lying in his tipi immediately before the two men take him to the sky and again upon his return: "As I entered the tipi I saw a boy lying there dying and I stood there awhile and finally found out that it was myself" (*The Sixth Grandfather* 142).

In *The Dakota or Sioux in Minnesota as They Were in 1834,* the Congregationalist missionary, Samuel W. Pond assumed that the subjects of his inquiry believed literally in their rituals, since they were primitive people and could not be expected to understand metaphors. This is pointedly exemplified in Pond's description of the Medicine Dance in which participants appeared to be "shot" by small objects passing from the inside of a medicine bag into their bodies. The shot would knock them down, and after an interval they would come to and cough up the object. Pond explains with well meant sympathy for the intelligence of the Dakota spectators: "Doubtless many of the spectators found it difficult to believe such palpable absurdities but there was nothing to be gained by publishing their skeptical thoughts, for it was not a light thing to incur the displeasure of some of the *wakan* men" (95). Gary Clayton Anderson retrospectively puts it in another light: "the ceremony was a ritual, supported by a belief system in which objects and acts represented a deeper spiritual truth, a fact that Pond failed to understand. (Pond did not have any difficulty in respecting the notion that during the Christian rite of Holy Communion, bread and wine represent the body and blood of Christ)" (Intro., S. Pond xv).

Despite his genuine respect for many aspects of the Dakota character, Pond cannot overcome his inability to perceive the metaphorical character of Dakota consciousness. In one of many instances he fails to understand a Dakota weather metaphor as being conventionally humorous: "They had an absurd way of accounting for the wane of the moon, saying that it was eaten up. The moon-eater seemed quite unequal to the task assigned him, for he was nothing more than a little mouse of a peculiar form, a species found occasionally though rather rarely in this country. How much credence this queer fancy gained among the Dakotas is uncertain, for, when bantered about it, they laughed and did not seem to care whether it was true or not" (S. Pond 84).

Lakota rituals that heal the body simultaneously heal the spirit by transforming fear and vulnerability into confidence. The patient beholds a symbolic change and empathetically receives the strength of the bear or other spirit transmitted by the administering specialist. But some dreamers enact a dramatic representation of their power without the immediate purpose of physical cure. Like the *heyoka* ceremony Black Elk's elk ceremony is a *wakan kaga,* a non-curative ritual of the type described by Powers (*Sacred Language* 183–86). Four virgins and six elk dreamers perform a unique play within an extensive repertoire of symbolic drama. The themes are presented in a distinctive way and the central symbol of the elk is present only in this ceremony:

They [the participants] went out of the tipi; the virgins first—the one with the pipe first, the one with the sacred stick next, the one with the herb [next], the [one with] the sacred hoop last. All of the virgins faced the west now, standing together. Then we six men came out snorting and acting like elks, stamping our feet. We all carried an eagle feather and some sage with us. One of the six elks carried a drum. The four virgins offered the relics to the west and then proceeded on to the north. As the virgins went the men danced around them like elks. (*The Sixth Grandfather* 243)

The energy in the men is inseparable from its source and is also visible in the sacred symbols "carried" or valued by virginal minds focused on their meaning. The beholders see and are realized as what they see. Each person's vitality depends upon their establishment of these priorities, the spontaneous return of attention to the meaning and use of the pipe, to the sacred stick, the herb, and the nation's hoop. The center, unique to this ceremony, manifests the abundance of spirit sources, in this case the elk, but implicitly all the other animal spirits favoring selected dreamers. The ceremony concludes as had the horse dance, with a return to the preparations tipi where "we could see tracks of all kinds of animals in there—spirit tracks" (*The Sixth Grandfather* 244). Neihardt omits this, perhaps to avoid redundancy after the horse dance, but losing the Lakota emphasis on the fulfillment of ceremonial expression. Rituals attract helping spirits who leave their tracks directly as if to confirm their acceptance of the kinship offered in human dance and song.

The contemporary Western mind is generally unable to conceive of miracles apart from melodramatic physical change in steadily paraded "wonders" from radios to rocketry. Literal belief in the spectacular displays of parting the red sea or keeping a bottle full are still matters of serious dispute in religious circles. A writer may think of the sudden occurrence of a good idea for a story as a miracle, and many creative people live familiarly in a world of such unexpected gifts. The Lakota world was especially receptive to vision in symbolic forms because its thinking was, as a rule, more metaphorical than that of our society, though not fundamentally different from that of creative individuals in any society. The Elk ceremony is an allegory of creativity itself. It has no purpose beyond that of serious Western art—to reflect and affirm its own process of coming into being and to suggest in the "tracks" it leaves that the audience follow the same path. The pipe is the basic means of extending one's metaphorical potential, first in its own meaning as a link between the individual and his larger humanity, then in the qualities of a fulfilled spirit represented by the directions to which it points. The spirit thus completes its cycle of growth in the sacred circuit in order to give new life, with the sacred stick and the herb as the means, and the sacred hoop as the result.

A *wicaśa wakan* is chosen by the spirits to speak their intent rather than his own. Faulkner said of two of his longest, most complex works, *The Sound and the Fury* and *Light in August,* that he had no idea what would happen to the characters before he sat down to write each day. Ben Jonson said of Shakespeare that he never blotted a line. Mozart composed finished pieces at the age of four, something no four year old should be able to do. These are exceptional phenomena in a culture which prefers that miracles validate security (salvation). Healing lepers, turning water into wine, or providing an inexhaustible food supply prove the desirability of coming under the wing of a master. Lakota ceremonies also heal, but the emphasis is on infusing strength within the person rather than shielding him. When a spirit helper given to a man in a vision is summoned to assist him in battle, he feels its strength within himself. In the same way outside spirits transmit strength through a symbolic medium, naturally or humanly shaped. Power is circulated, sent by the spirits as inspiration, returned to them as expression, and passed as easily through fiction as through "truth."

To return to Vine Deloria, Jr.'s dismissal of difference between Neihardt and Black Elk posed in the introduction: "Can it matter" when both men deliver the same inspired message? Deloria's universalism might also be applied to the question of ethnographic truth. Did the holy man lie, since many of his professed beliefs are contradictory? Drawing on a wide range of religious metaphors, some of them Christian, Black Elk spoke to protect the people. Under extraordinary historical circumstances, credal consistency and factual truth can hardly matter, but surely Black Elk has shown us what does.

WORKS CITED

Adams, John Quincy. *Memoirs of John Quincy Adams*. Ed. Charles Francis Adams. Philadelphia, 1875.

Allison, E. H. "The Stone Boy and the Spider." Handwritten ms. in the National Anthropological Archives, Smithsonian Institution, Washington, D.C.

Aly, Lucile F. "Trappers and Indians—Neihardt's Short Stories." *A Sender of Words: Essays in Memory of John G. Neihardt*. Salt Lake City: Howe Brothers, 1984. 72–84.

Ambrose, Stephen E. *Crazy Horse and Custer*. New York: Doubleday, 1975.

Amiotte, Arthur, "Eagles Fly Over." *Parabola* 1.3 (1976): 28–41.

———. "The Lakota Sun Dance: Historical and Contemporary Perspectives." In *Sioux Indian Religion*. Ed. Raymond J. DeMallie and Douglas R. Parks. Norman: U of Oklahoma P, 1987. 75–89.

———. "Our Other Selves: The Lakota Dream Experience." *Parabola* 7.2 (1982): 26–32.

Around Him, John, and Albert White Hat, Sr. *Lakota Ceremonial Songs*. Pierre: State Publishing, 1983.

Baker, Herschel. *The Image of Man: A Study of the Idea of Human Dignity in Classical Antiquity, the Middle Ages, and the Renaissance*. New York: Harper & Brothers, 1961.

Barsh, Russell Lawrence. "Contemporary Marxist Theory and Native American Reality." *American Indian Quarterly* 12.3 (1988): 187–212.

Bateson, Gregory. *Steps to an Ecology of Mind*. New York: Ballantine Books, 1972.

Black, W. E. "Ethic and Metaphysic: A Study of John G. Neihardt." *Western American Literature* 2.3 (1969): 205–12.

Black Elk. *Black Elk Speaks*. As told through John G. Neihardt. Intro. Vine Deloria, Jr. Lincoln: U of Nebraska P, 1979.

———. *The Sacred Pipe: Black Elk's Account of the Seven Rites of the Oglala Sioux.* Ed. Joseph Epes Brown. New York: Penguin, 1971.

———. *The Sixth Grandfather: Black Elk's Teachings Given to John G. Neihardt.* Ed. Raymond J. DeMallie. Lincoln: U of Nebraska P, 1984.

Blish, Helen. *A Pictographic History of the Oglala Sioux.* Lincoln: U of Nebraska P, 1967.

Buechel, Eugene, S. J., ed. *Lakota Tales and Texts.* Pine Ridge, SD: Red Cloud Lakota Langugage and Cultural Center, 1978.

———. "Notebook" March and April, 1915. Milwaukee: Holy Rosary Mission Records. H.R.M. Series 5, Box 1, Department of Special Collections and University Archives, Marquette University.

Bunge, Robert. *An American Urphilosophie: An American Philosophy BP (Before Pragmatism).* Lanham, MD: U P of America, 1984.

Castro, Michael. *Interpreting the Indian: Twentieth Century Poets and the Native American.* Albuquerque: U of New Mexico P, 1983.

Cave, Alfred E. "Canaanites in a Promised Land: The American Indian and the Providential Theory of Empire." *American Indian Quarterly* 12.4 (1988): 277–98.

Chittenden, Hiram M, and Alfred T. Richardson. *The Life, Letters, and Travels of Father Pierre Jean De Smet, S.J. 1801–1873. Missionary Labors and Adventures Among the Wild Tribes of the North American Indians.* 4 vols. 1905; rpt. New York: Arno Press, 1969.

Deloria, Ella C. *Dakota Texts.* 1932; rpt. New York: AMS Press, 1974.

———. *Speaking of Indians.* Vermillion, SD: State Publishing, 1983.

———. *Teton Myths* (The George Bushotter Collection). ca. 1937; Philadelphia: MS 30 (x8c.3), Boas Collection, American Philosophical Society.

Deloria, Vine, Jr. *The Metaphysics of Modern Existence.* New York: Harper & Rowe, 1979.

DeMallie, Raymond J. "Lakota Belief and Ritual in the Nineteenth Century." *Sioux Indian Religion*. Ed. Raymond J. DeMallie and Douglas R. Parks. Norman: U of Oklahoma P, 1987. 25–43.

———. "John G. Neihardt's Lakota Legacy." *A Sender of Words: Essays in Memory of John G. Neihardt*. Salt Lake City: Howe Brothers, 1984. 110–34.

Densmore, Frances. "Songs of the Sioux." LP Recording AFS L23. Washington: Library of Congress, 1951.

———. *Teton Sioux Music*. 1918; rpt. New York: Da Capo, 1972.

Dombrowski, Daniel A. "Black Elk's Platonism." *North Dakota Quarterly* 55.1 (1987): 56–64.

Dorsey, James O. *A Study of Siouan Cults*. 1894; rpt. Seattle: Shorey, 1972.

Drinnon, Richard. *Facing West: The Metaphysics of Indian-Hating and Empire-Building*. New York: New American Library, 1980.

Eastman, Mary. *Dahcotah: or Life and Legends of the Sioux around Fort Snelling*. New York, 1849.

Eliade, Mircea. *The Myth of the Eternal Return or Cosmos and History*. Princeton: Princeton U P, 1974.

Fletcher, Alice Cunningham. "Emblematic Use of the Tree in the Dakotan Group." *Proceedings of the American Association for the Advancement of Science* 45 (1897).

Fools Crow, Frank. "Fools Crow." LP Recording TLP 100. Denver: Tatanka Records, 1977.

———. Interviewed by Ed McGaa (8–30–67). Tape and Transcript no. 453. Vermillion: American Indian Research Project, South Dakota Oral History Center, U of South Dakota.

———. Interviewed by Mary Pat Cuny (9–21–74). Tape and Transcript no. 1243. Vermillion: American Indian Research Project, South Dakota Oral History Center, U of South Dakota.

Frye, Roland Mushat. *Shakespeare and Christian Doctrine*. Princeton: Princeton U P, 1963.

Graham, W. A. *The Custer Myth: A Source Book of Custeriana*. New York: Bonanza Books, 1953.

Hassrick, Royal B. *The Sioux: Life and Customs of a Warrior Society.* Norman: U of Oklahoma P, 1964.

Hawthorne, Nathaniel. *The Scarlet Letter.* New York: New American Library, 1959.

Holler, Clyde. "Black Elk's Relationship to Christianity." *American Indian Quarterly* 8.1 (1984): 37–49.

———. "Lakota Religion and Tragedy: The Theology of *Black Elk Speaks.*" *Journal of the American Academy of Religion* 52.1 (1984): 19–43.

Hyde, George E. *Spotted Tail's Folk: A History of the Brulé Sioux.* Norman: U of Oklahoma P, 1974.

Jahner, Elaine. "Stone Boy: Persistent Hero." *Smoothing the Ground: Essays on Native American Oral Literature.* Ed. Brian Swann. Berkeley: U of California P, 1983. 171–86.

Jacolliot, Louis S.J. *The Bible in India: Hindoo Origin of Hebrew and Christian Revelation.* New York, 1887.

Kadlecek, Edward and Mabell. *To Kill an Eagle: Indian Views on the Last Days of Crazy Horse.* Boulder: Johnson Books, 1981.

Krupat, Arnold. *For Those Who Come After: A Study of Native American Autobiography.* Berkeley: U of California P, 1985.

Laubin, Gladys and Reginald. *Indian Dances of North America: Their Importance to Indian Life.* Norman: U of Oklahoma P, 1977.

Mails, Thomas. *Fools Crow.* Lincoln: U of Nebraska P, 1990.

———. *Sundancing at Rosebud and Pine Ridge.* Sioux Falls: Augustana College, 1978.

Milton, John. *The Complete Poetry.* Ed. John T. Shawcross. Garden City, N.Y.: Doubleday, 1971.

Momaday, N. Scott. "To Save a Great Vision." *A Sender of Words: Essays in Memory of John G. Neihardt.* Salt Lake City: Howe Brothers, 1984. 30–38.

Mooney, James. *The Ghost-Dance Religion and the Sioux Outbreak of 1890.* 1896; rpt. Chicago: U of Chicago P, 1976.

Neihardt, John G. *The Divine Enchantment.* New York: James T. White & Co., 1900.

———. *The Song of the Indian Wars* and *The Song of the Messiah.* In *The Twilight of the Sioux.* Lincoln: U of Nebraska P, 1971.

————. Preface. *Black Elk Speaks*. New York: Pocket Books, 1972.

Novak, Michael. *The Spirit of Democratic Capitalism*. New York: Simon & Schuster, 1983.

Olson, Paul A. "Black Elk Speaks as Epic and Ritual Attempt to Reverse History." *Vision and Refuge: Essays on the Literature of the Great-Plains*. U of Nebraska P, 1982. 3–27.

Pearce, Roy Harvey. *The Savages of America: A Study of the Indian and the Idea of Civilization*. Baltimore: The Johns Hopkins U P, 1965.

Pond, Gideon H. "Dakota Superstitions." *Collections of the Minnesota Historical Society*. Saint Paul, 1867.

Pond, Samuel W. *The Dakota or Sioux in Minnesota as They Were in 1834*. 1908; rpt. St. Paul: Minnesota Historical Society Press, 1986.

Poole, D. C. *Among the Sioux of Dakota: Eighteen Months' Experience as an Indian Agent 1869–70*. 1881; rpt. St. Paul: Minnesota Historical Society Press, 1988.

Powers, Marla N. *Oglala Women: Myth, Ritual, and Reality*. Chicago: U of Chicago P, 1986.

Powers, William K. *Beyond the Vision: Essays on American Indian Culture*. Norman: U of Oklahoma P, 1987.

————. *Oglala Religion*. Lincoln: U of Nebraska P, 1975.

————. *Sacred Language: The Nature of Supernatural Discourse in Lakota*. Norman: U of Oklahoma P, 1986.

————. *Yuwipi: Vision and Experience in Lakota Ritual*. Lincoln: U of Nebraska P, 1982.

Ramsey, Jarold. *Reading the Fire: Essays in the Traditional Indian Literatures of the Far West*. Lincoln: U of Nebraska P, 1983.

Rice, Julian. *Lakota Storytelling: Black Elk, Ella Deloria, and Frank Fools Crow*. New York: Peter Lang, 1989.

Sandner, Donald. *Navajo Symbolic Healing*. New York: Harcourt, Brace, Jovanovich, 1979.

Sandoz, Mari. *Crazy Horse: The Strange Man of the Oglalas*. Lincoln: U of Nebraska P, 1961.

Schoolcraft, Henry Rowe. *Algic Researches*. New York, 1839.

Starkloff, Carl J., S.J. "Renewing the Sacred Hoop." *A Sender of Words: Essays in Memory of John G. Neihardt*. Salt Lake City: Howe Brothers, 1984. 159–72.

Steinmetz, Paul B., S.J. *Pipe, Bible, and Peyote among the Oglala Lakota*. Stockholm Studies in Comparative Religion 19. Motala, Sweden, 1980.

Steltenkamp, Michael Francis. "No More Screech Owl: Plains Indian Adaptation as Profiled in the Life of Black Elk," diss., Michigan State U, 1987.

Stolzman, William, S. J. *The Pipe and Christ: A Christian-Sioux Dialogue*. Pine Ridge, S.D.: Red Cloud Indian School, 1986.

Thoreau, Henry. *Writings*. Manuscript Edition, 16:251–52. Quoted in Roy Harvey Pearce, *The Savages of America: A Study of the Indian and the Idea of Civilization*. Baltimore: The Johns Hopkins U P, 1965. 149.

Vestal, Stanley. *Sitting Bull: Champion of the Sioux*. Norman: U of Oklahoma P, 1980.

———. *Warpath: The True Story of the Fighting Sioux Told in a Biography of Chief White Bull*. Lincoln: U of Nebraska P, 1984.

Walker, James R. *Lakota Belief and Ritual*. Ed. Raymond J. DeMallie and Elaine A. Jahner. Lincoln: U of Nebraska P, 1980.

———. *Lakota Myth*. Ed. Elaine A. Jahner. Lincoln: U of Nebraska P, 1983.

———. *Lakota Society*. Ed. Raymond J. DeMallie. Lincoln: U of Nebraska P, 1982.

———. *The Sun Dance and Other Ceremonies of the Oglala Division of the Teton Dakota*. 1917; rpt. New York: AMS Press, 1979.

Whitney, Blair. *John G. Neihardt*. New York: Twayne, 1976.

Wissler, Clark. "Societies and Ceremonial Associations in the Oglala Division of the Teton-Dakota." *Anthropological Papers of the American Museum of Natural History* 11 (1912): 1–99.

INDEX

Adams, John, 33, 34
Adams, John Quincy, 33
Anderson, Gary Clayton, 150
Anog-Ite (female Double-face), 133
Aryan, 17, 34

Baker, Herschel, 29–31
Bateson, Gregory, 16–17
Bear healers, 69, 75–79, 83–84, 150
Big Foot. See Sitanka
Black Elk, Benjamin, 13–14
Black Elk, ("Nicholas"): as Christian thinker and catechist, ix–xi, xiii, 1–10, 12–13, 104, 145–46; Dog (Thunder being) vision of, 69–72, 92, 112; as Ghost dancer, 5, 96; Great Vision of, xii, 20, 68, 70, 71, 74, 75, 90, 92, 112, 113, 114, 118, 123, 124, 125–26, 127–28, 136–37, 143–44, 145, 146, 149; as healer, xi, xiii, 1–2, 3, 9, 23, 76, 80, 84–86, 87–88, 118, 125, 144; as Lakota thinker, ix–xi, xii–xiii, 3–4, 5–6, 8–10, 13, 20, 24, 25, 28–30, 51, 59–60, 70–72, 88, 92, 104, 125–26, 136–38, 144, 146, 148–53; narrator of "Sharp Nose, the Arapahoe," xii–xiii, 11, 148; as Thunder dreamer, xii, xiii, 20, 28, 138–39, 146–47; as warrior, 12, 23, 94, 98, 101, 106
Black Elk, and John G. Neihardt, *Black Elk Speaks,* ix–xi, xiii, 4, 15–16, 19–21, 26–31, 48–49, 58–59, 61, 63–64, 70–72, 112, 124, 144, 146–47, 151

Black Elk, and Joseph Epes Brown, *The Sacred Pipe,* xi, 4, 5–9, 12, 62–63, 145, 149
Black, power of, xii, xiii, 8, 68, 114, 122, 145
Black road, 7, 8, 145–47
Blue man, 76, 84, 85
Brother-sister relation, 104–5, 109–11
Brown, Joseph Epes, xi, 1, 4, 7
Buffalo, xii, xiii, 7, 11, 12, 13, 66–67, 69, 94, 108, 109–10, 125–43, 146
Buffalo ceremony: girl's puberty, 126, 128, 129, 134–36; healing, xii, 100, 136–38
Buffalo chips, 128, 131
Buffalo dance, 132–34, 139
Buffalo fat, 130
Buffalo horns, 127, 129, 133, 134, 135, 137
Buffalo men, 132–33
Buffalo penis, 131
Buffalo skull, 127, 128, 132, 133, 134, 136, 139, 141, 142–43
Buffalo tongues, 129
Buffalo women, 128, 129, 134–36
Bushotter, George, 75, 76, 94, 96

Caesar, Julius (Shakespearean character), 15, 47, 53, 54, 56
Calvin, John, 44
Campbell, Joseph, x, 25
Catches, Paul, 5
Catches, Pete, Sr., 5, 90
Chokecherry juice, 135
Clay, Henry, 33, 34

Cody, Buffalo Bill, 1, 54
Colossians (3: 9–11), 47, 49, 62
Crazy Buffalo (Gnaśki), 114, 130, 131, 135, 137, 140
Crazy Horse, xii, 10, 11, 20, 27, 68, 93–94, 98, 105, 138–39, 140; as portrayed in *Black Elk Speaks*, 27; as portrayed in *The Song of the Indian Wars*, 19–20, 56–57

Deloria, Vine, Jr., 15–18, 152
DeMallie, Raymond J. Introduction to *The Sixth Grandfather*, ix, xii, 1, 2–3, 4, 5, 12, 20, 23, 25, 61–63, 76, 112, 123–24; "Lakota Legacy," 18–19, 48–49, 60–62
Dogs: in Bear healing, 78; in Black Elk's Dog vision, 71–72, 124; in Black Elk's Great Vision, 126; in Black Elk's *heyoka* ceremony, 72–73; in "Miwakan Yuhala," 102–4
Dombrowski, Daniel A., 26–28
Double-face, 99–100, 103, 104, 105, 108
Drinks Water: in *The Sixth Grandfather*, 28–29, 58–59, 63; in *Black Elk Speaks*, 58–59. *See also* Wooden Cup
Drinnon, Richard, 34–35
Duhamel pageant, 4

Eagles, 71, 76, 98, 101, 105, 113, 137, 138, 142–43, 145
Eagle Wing Stretches, 91, 92, 104
Ear piercing, of children, 132–33
Eliot, T. S., 17
Elk: ceremony, 150–51; power of, 13, 124, 150–51
Emerson, Ralph Waldo, 22
Erasmus, 31

Faulkner, William, 24, 152
Fear, value of, 68–74, 75–79, 114, 115–17, 131, 135, 146, 150

Femininity, Lakota concepts of, 139–45
Flaming Rainbow, 124
Fools Crow, Frank, 77, 80, 85, 87, 115–17, 118, 149
Franklin, Benjamin, 33, 34
Freud, Sigmund, 26
Frye, Northrop, 24

Ghost dance, 5, 6, 18, 47, 48, 51–52, 70
"The Gift of the Horse," 117–20, 122
Gnaśki. See Crazy Buffalo
Good Seat, 87, 90

Hairy Chin, 75
Hanbleceya (the vision quest), 36, 40, 69–72, 75, 92, 126, 129, 140, 141, 142, 145, 146, 149, 150
Hanson, Charles, 4
Hawthorne, Nathaniel, x, 43, 45–47, 55
Healing, Lakota, xi, xiii, 75–88, 125, 136–38, 143–44, 150, 152
Helpers, supernatural, xi, 79, 83–86, 87, 92–98, 105–6, 140, 149, 152
Helper stories: "Miwakan Yuhala" 'Sword Owner,' xi, 94–104; "Hokśila Wan" 'A Boy,' 104–11
Heyoka, 38, 69, 104, 115, 130; ceremony, 72–73, 86–87, 149, 150
Hmu, 100, 108
"Hokśila Wan" 'A Boy.' See Helper stories
Holler, Clyde, 5, 6, 23–24
Hooker, Richard, 44
Horses, 13, 68, 70, 82, 110, 139, 145; as carrying the power of the Thunder, 112–13, 114–20, 122–24, 126, 144, 145
Horse dance, 27–28; Black Elk's, 68–69, 70, 71, 72, 73, 75, 112, 113, 114, 115, 122, 123, 136, 142, 149, 151; Fools Crow's, 115–17

Hunka ceremony, 38, 114, 126, 127, 133, 139, 141–42

Iktomi, 82, 89, 129, 133, 135, 140
Inyan (the Rock), 120
Iya, 129–30, 131

Jacolliot, Louis, S. J.: *The Bible in India,* 21
Judaism, 5, 31, 32, 37–40, 41
Jung, Carl G., x, 26

Keaton, William H., 32
Krupat, Arnold, 24

Laubin, Reginald and Gladys, 4
Light, Christian metaphor of, 44–46, 49, 50, 54, 57–58, 59, 65
Lindebner, Joseph S. J., 2
Little Wound, 88
Lone Goose, John, 4
Lone Man, 115
Longfellow, Henry Wadsworth, 33
Looks Twice, Lucy, 2, 4, 5, 13
Lynd, James W., 88

Manifest Destiny, 21, 31, 54
Marrowbone, Ben, 5
Marxism, 24, 25, 26
Masculinity, Lakota concepts of, 102–3, 140–45
"Materialist" religion, 37–38
"Maturity," religious, 21–22, 31–34, 36, 41–42, 48–49
Menstruation, 144
Metaphor, Lakota concepts of, 148–53
Milton, John, x, xiii, 36, 43–44, 46, 49
"Miwakan Yuhala" 'Sword Owner.' *See* Helper stories
Moles, 93, 142
Monotheism, Lakota, 88, 129
Mooney, James, 51
Morgan, Lewis Henry, 32

Nagi, 87, 90
Nagila, 87, 90
Natural Christians, 37, 41, 44
Neihardt, John G., ix–xi, xiii, 1, 4, 7, 8, 9, 10, 12, 15, 17–25, 26–27, 31–32, 33–34, 36, 40, 59, 65, 76, 85, 92, 112, 113, 121, 124, 144, 146–47, 151; as Christian poet, x, xi, xiii, 7, 8, 13, 15–16, 18–23, 24–25, 28, 29, 30–31, 41–42, 44, 46, 48–58, 61, 62–63; and *Black Elk Speaks. See* Black Elk and John G. Neihardt, *Black Elk Speaks;* and *The Divine Enchantment,* 21–22; and "The Singer of the Ache," 22–23; and *The Song of the Indian Wars,* 19–20, 43, 56–57; and *The Song of the Messiah,* 18–19, 22, 30, 36, 43, 48–56, 57, 61; and *When the Tree Flowered,* 15; and "The White Wakunda," 23
Niya, 87, 90, 108, 111

Oglala Horse Society, 122
One Side, 137
Ordeal, value of, 70–72, 73–74, 78–79, 81–85, 86–87, 92–111, 113–24
Orthography, Lakota, 95–96n

Pearce, Roy Harvey, 31
Peckham, Sir George, 43
Pipe, 5, 42, 74, 81, 119, 127, 128, 130, 131, 134, 135, 137, 140, 144, 151
The Pipe and Christ. See Stolzman, William S. J.
Platonism, 7, 16, 19, 22, 26–29, 30, 31
Pond, Gideon, 89–90
Pond, Samuel W., 65, 88, 89, 149–50
Poor Thunder, 115–16, 117, 118
Powers, William K., 42, 90, 92, 150
Pte (buffalo cow and generic term), 141

Racism, 17–19, 34

Rainbow, 68, 96, 124, 125, 126, 127, 132, 148

Rattling Hawk, 78

Red, power of, xii, xiii, 101, 125, 127–28, 130, 132, 133, 134–38, 144–45, 146, 147

Red Cloud, 10; as portrayed in *The Song of the Messiah,* 58–59

Red Dog, 136–38

Red road, 7, 8, 136–37, 145, 146, 147

Reincarnation, Dakota belief in, 89–91

Ritual, purpose and value of, 23, 25, 31, 36, 37, 65–74, 75–86, 93, 94, 98, 105–6, 108, 130, 149–51, 152

Roosevelt, Theodore, 34

Salvation, Christian, xi, 7–8, 16, 24–25, 28, 29, 30–31, 36–40, 43, 44, 45, 49–52, 54–56, 61–63, 65, 104

Sage, 135, 136

Sexuality; in the sun dance, 129–32; in the Buffalo woman ceremony, 135–36

"Sharp Nose, the Arapahoe." *See* Black Elk, narrator of

Sherman, William T., 34

Shooter, 80

Sicun: as power, 79–80, 82, 86, 87–88, 93, 98, 105, 112, 118; as innate part of a person, 87, 90, 105

Sitanka (Big Foot), as portrayed in *The Song of the Messiah,* 48–50, 55–56

Sitting Bull, 11, 20, 29–30; as portrayed in *The Song of the Indian Wars,* 46, 52–54

Śkan, 121

Sneak-up dance, 114

Sodalities, Roman Catholic, 2

Soldier weed, 112, 121

Song of the Indian Wars. See John G. Neihardt

Song of the Messiah. See John G. Neihardt

Soul, Christian immortality of, xi, 5, 16, 28, 30, 36–37, 39, 43, 62–63, 126–27, 146

Soul: Lakota concepts of, 87, 90, 91; Lakota immortality of, 87, 89–90, 93; reincarnation of, 89–91

Spotted Tail, 10–11, 12; as portrayed in *Black Elk Speaks,* 10–11

Starkloff, Carl J., S. J., 42, 43, 56, 60, 64, 65

Steltenkamp, Michael F., 4–5, 145–46

Stolzman, William, S. J., 33, 36–41, 47, 65

Stones, 80, 85, 93, 142, 149

Sucking cure, 81–82, 84, 86

Sun dance, 6, 87, 113–14, 126, 127–33, 134, 135, 136, 137, 139, 141, 142–43, 144–45, 146

Swallows, 113, 116, 124, 126, 141

Sweat lodge, 38, 70, 72, 87, 105, 139, 140, 142, 149

Sweetgrass, 83, 128, 133, 136

Sword, George, 79, 88, 109

Tattoo, 87

Tecumseh, 48

Thoreau, Henry David, 32

Thunder, power of, xii, 12, 20, 28, 68–73, 76, 84, 92, 94, 96, 112–13, 114–24, 125–26, 127, 138–39, 142, 144, 146–47

Thunder bird. *See* Wakinyan

Ton, 88, 123

Tonwan, 112, 116, 118, 123

Transcendentalism, 22, 23

Tribal religion, 20, 23, 25–28, 30–32, 38–40, 47

Tyon, Thomas, 77, 78

Twain, Mark, 17, 34

INDEX

Universalist religion, Christianity
  as, 18, 20, 21–22, 23, 36–40,
  46–47, 48–49, 51–52, 55, 62–63

Virgins, 143–45, 150–51
Virtues, Lakota: male, 116–17, 128,
  140, 142; female, 140, 142
Vision quest. See *Hanbleceya*

Wakan kaga (sacred non-curative performance), 150
Wakinyan, 114–15, 116, 120–22,
  124
Wamakaśkan (spirit animals), 93
Water, power of, 84–86, 118, 121,
  139

White Buffalo Calf (pipe) Woman,
  109, 110, 139, 142, 144, 145
White Bull, Joseph, 11–12, 94
Whitney, Blair, 22
Winkte (man who lives as woman),
  101
Wooden Cup, 59–60, 63
"Worn" (by a spirit), 138
Wounded Knee, 44, 49–50, 61, 98,
  101, 139

Yumni, 129
Yuwipi, 86

Zimmerman, Joseph, S. J., 42